THE BACCHAE

Also translated by Donald Sutherland:

Lysistrata (1961)

Hippolytus in Drama and Myth (With an essay by
    Hazel E. Barnes) (1960)

THE BACCHAE
OF EURIPIDES

A new translation with a critical essay
by Donald Sutherland

UNIVERSITY OF NEBRASKA PRESS · LINCOLN

Publishers on the Plains

UNP

Manufactured in the United States of America

To Chet and Crit

Foreword

Since the Greek text contains no indications about staging and scenery except those one may infer from the speeches, all stage directions have been supplied by the translator. However, many details of the staging are highly problematical, and their discussion has been relegated to notes at the end of the play. The many interpolations, necessary to a stageable version, are indicated by brackets in the text of the translation, the longest and most important being discussed in the notes.

Not only the general interpretation of the play but the expression of individual speeches is controversial. The translator's interpretation inevitably colors the wording of the text to some degree, but rarely appears in the stage directions. An essay on that interpretation, involving stylistics and the "motivation" of lines, is appended, for the convenience of directors and actors and the curiosity of readers.

The numbers in parentheses in the margin of the play refer to notes beginning on page 82. The numbers at the top of the pages of play text correspond approximately to the line numbers of the original Greek text.

D.S.

Contents

THE BACCHAE

Dramatis Personae

DIONYSUS
TIRESIAS
CADMUS
PENTHEUS
GUARD (*Messenger*)
HERDSMAN (*Messenger*)
HOUSE-SLAVE (*Messenger*)
AGAVE

CHORUS *of Asiatic Bacchants*
MUTE ATTENDANTS, *male and perhaps some female*

SCENE: *Before the outer gate of the palace of Pentheus*
TIME: *Mythological*

Prologue

(Enter DIONYSUS *disguised as an effeminate priest.)*

DIONYSUS:

    I come, a child of Zeus, again to Thebes
    where once King Cadmus' daughter, Semele,
    bore me, Dionysus, whom she had by Zeus,
    delivered of me by the lightning's fire.
    Changing my godhead for a mortal shape
    I walk by Dirce's springs, Ismenus' wave,
    and see my thunderstricken mother's tomb
    there by the palace, and those smoking ruins,
    the flame of Zeus' fire that yet lives on,
    Hera's immortal outrage and revenge
    against my mother. Cadmus did very well
    to consecrate that ground and make of it
    his daughter's shrine and unapproachable,
    but it was I who screened it roundabout
    with clusters and fresh foliage of the vine.
    Leaving the golden tracts of Lydia
    and Phrygia for the sun-struck Persian plains,
    visiting too the Bactrian fastnesses,
    the storm-swept country of the Medes, then rich
    Arabia, and all Asia's briny shores,
    wherever she holds in fee the noble towers
    of many a barbarian city mixed with Greek,
    I come to Greece, and my own city first.
    Having set up my ritual dance abroad

and mysteries where I could show myself
in my true presence to mortals, I was yet
a power not honored on my native soil.
Here, in this land of Greece, I have made Thebes
the first to ring with cries to me, and hung
her flesh with fawnskins, placing in her hand
my sacred wand, the shaft with ivy entwined,
because my mother's own sisters have blasphemed,
who should have been the last to do so, saying
that Dionysus was not bred from Zeus,
that Semele, had by some mortal man,
put off on Zeus the error of her bed,
prompted by Cadmus, for whose cleverness
they gloatingly said that she was killed by Zeus,
because she claimed falsely to be his bride!
Now I have driven them raving from the house
by spurs of madness. Stricken out of their minds
they dwell deep in the mountains, forced to wear
the trappings and the emblems of my cult.
And likewise all the female stock of Thebes,
all who are women grown, I've driven forth
mad from their houses; they too, having joined
with Cadmus' daughters far among the cliffs,
sit upon open rock under green pines.
For Thebes must learn, whether she will or no,
in what crude ignorance of my mysteries
she has denied, on the ground of Semele,
my mother, a mortal, that I am a god
revealed to mortals, born by her to Zeus.
Now Cadmus has given over his royal power
to Pentheus, whom another daughter bore,

but who, where I'm concerned, defies the gods,
refusing me libations and in prayers
making of me no mention. I therefor
will show myself to him and to all Thebes
as born a god. When I have set things right
here, I shall pass into another land,
once I've revealed myself. But now, should Thebes
dare try with arms and anger to bring back
her Bacchae from the mountain, I must lead
troops of my Maenads into the attack—
for which I have assumed this mortal guise
and changed my true shape for the form of man.
But oh, my throng of women who have come
with me from Lydia, which Mount Tmolus guards,
you I have chosen from barbarian tribes
for adepts and companions of my way,
lift up your native Phrygian tambourines,
made first by the Great Mother and myself—
come round this palace of King Pentheus
and sound them, here, so the whole town may see,
while I go join those Bacchae in their dance,
to Mount Cithairon's gorges, where they are.

(*Exit* DIONYSUS; *enter* CHORUS *of Maenads.*)

CHORUS:

From an Orient land, far
from the high Tmolus we come, swift in a sweet labor
    for Bromius. Work done
for the bull-god with a bull's roar is a work that we call
    none.
Who is here? Let him stand far

from our path! Here in the street, there in the halls, let
there be consecrate stillness
as we sing hymns to our god, hymns he established and
timeless:
    Blessed the man whom divine choice
    trains in the mysteries,
    all his life long to rejoice,
    blissful and purified;
    hallowed, enraptured in spirit, he is
    one of the dance on the mountainside,
and the Great Mother Cybele's celebrations he attends,
crowned
with the live ivy, and leaps swinging the wand high, as
at each bound
he invokes lord Dionysus.
Onward, O Bacchae, onward, O Bacchae, conducting
the Thundering god,
born of a god, Dionysus,
down from the mountains of Phrygia home to the broad
streets of the broad cities of Greece, Dionysus.
    Once, in the pangs of a forced birth,
    struck by a thunderstorm
    sent by Zeus flaming to earth,
    dying Semele cast
    out of her womb a new god without form,
    leaving her life in the lightning's blast.
And at once Zeus got the child, hid it away deep in a
strange pit
of his own thigh, and with gold brooches he locked in
and he sealed it
from the shrewd searching of Hera.

Then, when the Fates had fashioned it, Zeus bore a
  god with the horns of a bull,
crowned him with garlands of terror,
garlands of snakes. Hence we fling round our ringlets a
  full
circlet of live serpents, the catch of the wearer.

Thebes! O blessed Semele's town,
crown your head with an ivy crown!
Flower and abound with the evergreen
smilax of beautiful berry and sheen!   *(1.)*
Be all a Bacchant! Swing your divine
branches of oak, branches of pine!
Put on skins of the dappled fawn!
Trim them with white wool flecks! Put on
most a religious mind: revere
violence done by the god's rods here!
Soon all the land will be dancing and singing
  our songs,
soon, when the Thunderer leads them in throngs
off to the mountain, off to the mountain, awaited
there by the women already elated,
looms and shuttles left far behind,
now Dionysus possesses and stings their mind.

— O Kuretës! Your sacred cave!—
hollows chosen to bear and save
Zeus in his infancy nursed in Crete,
while triple-plumed Korybantes beat
hard on this drum, whose tight leathern round
they were the first ever to sound,

7

keeping time with their bounding feet,
blending its beat with the loud and sweet
breath of the Phrygian flutes, and they
gave it to Rhea to keep one day.
Now to its pounding the cries of her revelers ring.
Once she was robbed of this coveted thing,
she the Great Mother, Rhea the goddess: unruly
Satyrs· got hold of it, passing it duly
on to us, for the winter rites,
dances wherein Dionysus in turn delights.

Sweet in the mountains to fall outrun by the throng in
    the full cry,
fall entranced, wearing the holy garment of fawnskin,
fall hunting the fresh blood of the slain goat and the
    ecstasy
of the raw feast we go racing to win
into the mountains of Phrygia, Lydia, happily led
by the Thunderer, first in the hunting-calls.
And the ground is flowing with white milk and flowing
    with red
wine and flowing with nectar of bees,
while a smoke as of Syrian incense falls
streaming away from the shaft shaken aloft to the
    breeze
by the priest possessed, lifting the glaring flash of a
    torch of pine
as he runs, driving the wanderers back to the dancing-
    line,
shouting, brandishing, hurling his hair
long and delicate high in the air.

He responds to their cries of joy with a roar:
Onward, O Bacchae, oh, onward, O Bacchae, the pride
of holy Tmolus whose gorges pour
rivers of gold! Come and adore
Dionysus with dance and song and a thunder of drums!
Let the god of joy in your shouts of joy be glorified,
as into the shrilling of Phrygian cries and calls there
   comes
the holy melodious flute, whose playful and holy sounds
wander with us to the mountains, the mountains, an air
   so sweet
the Bacchant stirs, like a filly at graze with a dam, her
   fleet
limbs, and giddily skips and bounds!

FIRST EPISODE

(*Enter* TIRESIAS, *the blind prophet, dressed up in dionysiac costume
and tapping his way to the gate of the palace with a thyrsus.*)

TIRESIAS:
   Is anyone at the gates, who will call forth
   old Cadmus from the house—Agenor's son,
   the man who once left Sidon's citadel
   to found this Thebes with towers? Go in, someone;
   tell him Tiresias wants him. He will know
   himself what I have come for, and what things,
   old as I am, I have agreed to do
   with him, who is even older—to fix up
   a thyrsus and to wear the pelts of fawns,
   wreathing my head in sprigs of ivy leaf.

CADMUS (*enters slowly from gate*):
  My dear old friend—for I knew that voice was yours
  as soon as ever I heard it here inside,
  an echo of wit announcing a wise man.
  Here *I* am, ready and waiting, having on
  this outfit of the god, because we should—
  he being a son born of a daughter of mine,
  [Dionysus, and a god revealed to man—]*
  magnify him so far as we have power.
  Where shall we dance? Where shall we do our steps
  and toss our hoary heads? Instruct me now,
  as one old man an older, for in such lore
  you are the wise one. Never, night or day,
  could I grow weary of beating on the ground
  the sacred staff. What pleasure to forget
  how old we are!
TIRESIAS: You feel as I do, then?
  I too grow young, and shall attempt the dance!
CADMUS:
  Let us ride out of town into the hills!
TIRESIAS:
  The god would have more honor if we walked.
CADMUS:
  At our age? *I* to walk *you* like a child?
TIRESIAS:
  The god will guide us there without fatigue.
CADMUS:
  Are we the only men in town to dance?

  * Line probably spurious and certainly to be omitted in production.

TIRESIAS:

We two alone are right, the others wrong.

CADMUS:

We are long starting. Hold onto my arm.

TIRESIAS:

There! Grip my hand. We'll hitch up like a team.

CADMUS:

Being but mortal, *I* do not scorn the gods.

TIRESIAS:

We do not try our wits upon the powers.
Traditions from our fathers, which we keep
as an inheritance as old as time,
no reasoning will ever overthrow,
not even if the quibble be contrived
by the highest intellect. People will ask
if I do not disgrace my years to go
dancing like this, with ivy on my head.
No, for the god did not distinguish who
must dance for him, the young man or the old,
but wants to have his honor from everyone,
from all in common, not at all to be
magnified only by a numbered few.

CADMUS:

Since you, Tiresias, do not see this light,
I'll be *your* prophet, and tell you the unseen.
Here towards the palace Pentheus comes in haste,
Echion's son, to whom I gave the crown.
How agitated he is! What news has he?

(*Enter* PENTHEUS *with a few* GUARDS. *He is wearing high*

11

heavy boots and a cloak, as returning from travel. He is no older
than adolescent, but big and powerfully built. At first he does not see
the old men.)

PENTHEUS:
    I happen to leave the country for a time,
    and now I hear of strange calamities
    all over town—our women leaving home
    on some pretext of mystic revelries
    to swarm the shadowed mountains, honoring
    with dances one who is suddenly a god—
    one Dionysus, whoever *he* may be . . .
    how mixing-bowls amongst the celebrants
    stand brimming, but each woman slinks away,
    scattering deeper into the wilderness
    to do her service—bedding down with men.
    They claim to be conducting services
    as Maenads of the god of wine; rather
    it's love and Aphrodite they adore.
    Those I have caught, my officers hold safe
    in public prisons, their hands bound with chains,
    and all those still at large I shall hunt down
    out of the mountains—even Agave,
    my mother, and Ino, and Autonoë,
    Actaeon's mother as well. Constraining them
    in hunting nets of iron, I'll put a stop
    to all their wicked raptures quickly enough!
    I hear too that a stranger has come to town,
    a quack, a singer of spells from Lydia,
    with tawny ringlets and his hair perfumed,
    complexion rosy with wine, and in his eyes

12

the charms of Aphrodite. Night and day
he mingles with the girls, luring them on
by festivals to Bacchus. But if I
get hold of him inside my palace here
I'll stop his pounding the thyrsus and tossing
those tresses high—by cutting off his head
clean from the shoulders. He's the one who says
that Dionysus is a god, and once,
says he, was sewn up in the thigh of Zeus,
the same who perished in the lightning's blaze,
together with his mother, for she lied,
saying Zeus had loved her. Do such outrageous tales
and conduct so outrageous not deserve
the deadly noose—whatever that stranger is?
But here's another marvel! I behold
that reader of prodigies, Tiresias,
dressed up in spotted fawnskins, and my own
grandfather, perfectly ridiculous,
cavorting with a wand! Sir, I do hate
to see your age so destitute of mind!
Shake off that ivy! Emancipate your hand
from that degrading stick!—My own mother's father!
You put him up to this, Tiresias!
You want to introduce this one god more
to men, so that more reading of the birds
and signs by fire will bring you in more pay!
If hoary age did not make you exempt,
you'd sit in chains among the Bacchae now,
for bringing in foul rituals. Once the gleam
of the grape occurs at a women's feast, I say
there's nothing healthy in their revels left!

CHORUS:

The blasphemy! Stranger, revere the gods,
and Cadmus too, who sowed the dragon's teeth
Echion   your father sprang from! You disgrace your breed!
spartae TIRESIAS:

If a wise man take up an excellent
ground for discourse, fine speech comes readily.
You *have* the voluble tongue of a wise man
but in your words there's no intelligence.
A bold man, if in power and eloquent,
can be at last the ruin of the state,
having no prudence. This new deity,
the one you now deride—my words would fail
expressing what a greatness throughout Greece
he soon will be. There are two things, young man,
first principles for mortals: Demeter, one,
a goddess. She is also Earth. Call her
whichever name you will. While she herself,
as grain, brings up mankind on what is dry,
he came, Semele's child, and countered this:
he found the wetness of the grape for drink,
and brought it to mankind. It stops the grief
of miserable mortals, once they are filled
with flowing of the vine, and it gives sleep,
forgetfulness of all their daily cares.
Unhappiness has no other medicine.
This god, poured out, propitiates the gods,
so men get all their happiness through him.
And such a god you find ridiculous,
as having been sewn up in the thigh of Zeus.
I will teach you how all that is very well.

14

Zeus, having snatched him from the lightning's fire,
to Olympus brought the fetus newly born,
and Hera meant to throw it out of heaven,
but Zeus answered her scheming by a scheme
worthy a god: he broke a little piece
out of the ether that surrounds the earth,
and made a hostage [of *that* glowing shape]*
to Hera's rancor, sending out [the true]*
Dionysus [to the mountain nymphs to nurse,
raised as the son upon the sly of Zeus].*
This turned to "sewn up in the thigh of Zeus,"
as mortals, after a while, mixed up the words,
and then interpreted. He's oracular,
this god, and his intoxication is,
like any madness, full of prophecy.
For when this deity in plenitude
enters the body, then his revelers rave,
revealing in their words what is to come.
And he assumes a certain part of war,
for when an army stands in battle array
panic will sometimes sweep it through and rout,
before it even sets hand to javelin.
That too is a madness Dionysus sends.
You'll see him yet upon the very crags
of Delphi, leaping along the double peaks
by torchlight, hurling, shaking his ritual stalk,
great throughout Hellas. Believe me, Pentheus:
don't flatter yourself the state controls mankind.

---

* Interpolations by translator to clarify a difficult and probably
corrupted passage.

If you must judge—when your judgment is not itself—
judge yourself not so very knowing a man:
welcome the god into the land and pour
libations to him, revel and wreathe your head.
It is not Dionysus who will force
women to virtue in regard to love,
but whether virtue every way abides
within their natures—that's what you should ask,
for even when she joins these revelries
the virtuous woman will not be seduced.
You know how you rejoice when many stand
about your gates and glorify the name
of Pentheus. Well, the god likes honor too.
But as for me, and Cadmus, whom you mock,
we'll top ourselves off with ivy and go dancing,
a hoary old pair, but still we have to dance.
I shall not, swayed by any words of yours,
do battle against the gods, for you are mad,
so agonizingly mad that neither by drugs
can you be cured, nor without them be so sick!

CHORUS:

Old man, Apollo is not discredited
by what you say; and honoring as well
our bellowing god you are wise, for he is great.

CADMUS:

My child, Tiresias has advised you well.
Stay home with us—inside our ancient ways.
Now you're upset. Thinking, you take no thought.
For even if, as you say, this god is not,
still tell yourself he is, tell a fine lie
that he *is* Semele's child, so she may seem

the mother of a god, and the honor accrue
to us, to all the family. Look out:
you have seen what a hard fate Actaeon's was,
whom the bloodthirsty hounds he raised himself
tore into pieces, who boasted he could hunt
better than Artemis in her own preserves.
And lest that happen to you—here!—I shall wreathe
your head with ivy. Honor the god with us!

PENTHEUS:

No! Do not touch me! Go reveling if you will,
but never wipe your nonsense off on me!
But from this tutor of yours in silliness
I shall have justice! March now, one of you,
out to that sanctuary where he reads
the cries of birds. Take crowbars; pry it apart;
heave the place over, turn it upside down;
hurl everything together in one heap;
abandon to the winds and to the gales
the sanctifying ribbons! By this act
I shall especially bite him to the quick!
You others, scour the city and track down
that stranger with the feminine looks who brings
on women a new disease, and fouls our beds.
And when you take him, bind him, bring him here
to get the public stoning he deserves,
and die, finding in Thebes a bitter revelry!
                    (*Exit.*)

TIRESIAS:

Savage! You are bewildered in your words!
Now you are really mad, distraught before!
Let us go, Cadmus, now, and let us pray

for that man, even if he *has* run wild,
and for the city, praying the god to do
nothing untoward. But come along with me,
bringing your ivied staff, and try to hold
my body upright, as I'll try to hold yours.
Two old men falling would be an ugly thing.
But what of that ? We still must serve like slaves
the reveling god who is the child of Zeus.
May Pentheus bring down nothing to repent,
Cadmus, upon your house. I do not speak
now as a prophet, but reading the plain facts:
a fool spells folly. That's a certain sign.

(*Exeunt.*)

CHORUS:
Holiness, goddess on high,
Holiness, over the wide
world on a gold wing as you fly,
do you hear what this king wants done ?
Do you hear his unholy pride,
his threats to the Thundering son
of Semele, the first of the blessed powers
in the festive pleasures adorned with flowers ?
In his gift is our coming together to dance,
and to laugh to the flute's exuberance,
and to cease from care, when the clustered vine
brings a gleam to the feast where immortals dine,
when in festivals decked with ivy that mortals keep
the wine-bowl finally wraps them round with sleep.

Mouths without bridles and bits,

minds without rule, without sense,
end in a brute ruin that fits.
But a life at a quiet pace,
of discretion and reverence,
remains unafflicted in place
and continues the breed of its house. From far
the Olympians watch what we mortals are,
and our wisdom is not of the intellect, not
in presuming too high for human thought.
Life is short. A man who pursues immense
speculations may find, for today's expense,
he has nothing in cash. To me, such a man is mad,
who will not reckon with time—his planning, bad.

Oh, to journey to Cyprus,
island of Aphrodite,
where, to divert and enchant us
mortals, the troops of the Cupids play!
There the Paphian land is made
rich by a hundred rainless streams
sent by the Nile. Or let me be
hence to the Muses' favorite place conveyed,
far to Pieria's height that seems
fairest of all, in solemnity
slanting down from Olympus.
Lead us, Thunderer, Bromius,
lead us dancing enraptured there.
There are the Graces.
There is the spirit of Longing. And there are the ritual
    places
you and your revelers all may share!

Zeus-begotten, our god who
favors the feast, the revel,
favors the goddess of Peace, too,
giver of bounty, of living well,
in whose keeping young men survive.
Equally blessing the rich, the poor,
he has conferred the joy of wine.
Yes, and he hates the mortal who will not strive
nightly and daily to find secure
pleasures and live out a life divine,
sagely keeping a plain mind,
far from those of the rarer kind.
Whatsoever the multitude,
ignorant, lowly,
once has established and practices faithfully, thinking it
    holy,
let me agree to it, call it good.

SECOND EPISODE

(*Enter* PENTHEUS *from palace. Then* DIONYSUS, *his hands bound,
and several* GUARDS, *from the side.*)

SOLDIER:
Pentheus, at your orders. We have caught
this quarry you sent us after. We had luck.
The beast here we found tame. He made no move
to escape, but willingly held out his hands.
His ruddy cheek did not alter or turn pale.
Laughing he told us to come on, bind him,
lead him away. He stood there waiting and made
the work I had to do as good as done.

Ashamed, I said, "I arrest you, stranger, not
of my own will, but under the command
of Pentheus, who sent me." However, sir,
those Bacchae you had seized and bound in chains,
shut in the public prison, now are gone;
unbound, they run leaping toward the wilderness,
calling upon the name of the roaring god.
The fetters of themselves fell from their feet;
the bars of the doors without a mortal touch
came loose. This man has come to Thebes here, packed
with miracles. We must leave the rest to you.

PENTHEUS:

Unbind his hands! Being within our nets
he is not so agile as to escape me now.
But bodily you are not bad looking, stranger,
in a seductive way—indeed you came
to Thebes for women. Those locks of yours are long,
for lack of sport, cascading along your cheek,
full of enticement. That light skin you get
not from the beating sun, but in the shade,
saving your beauty as a lure to love.
But tell me, first, who are you, as to race?

DIONYSUS:

That story is not long, but easily told:
no doubt you have heard of Tmolus' flowering heights?

PENTHEUS:

I have. They ring the city of Sardis round.

DIONYSUS:

I am from there. My country is Lydia.

PENTHEUS:

Then why do you bring these rituals into Greece?

21

DIONYSUS:

Dionysus shipped us here, the son of Zeus.

PENTHEUS:

Have you some *Lydian* Zeus, who breeds new gods?

DIONYSUS:

No, but the same who *here* wed Semele.

PENTHEUS:

Did he force this on you in dreams or wide awake?

DIONYSUS:

Awake, and gave me the sacred rites and signs.

PENTHEUS:

In what form are these rites and signs of yours?

DIONYSUS:

They're not for the uninitiate to know.

PENTHEUS:

But what good are they to the initiate?

DIONYSUS:

That is not for you to hear—yet good to know.

PENTHEUS:

You gild it well, to incite me to hear more!

DIONYSUS:

No. We abhor a zealous unbelief.

PENTHEUS:

You say you saw him plain. What was he like?

DIONYSUS:

Whatever he liked. I wasn't commanding that.

PENTHEUS:

Another good feint—and telling me not a thing!

DIONYSUS:

Talk sense to a dolt—he'll say you make no sense.

PENTHEUS:

Is this the first place you have brought your god?

DIONYSUS:

Already all Asia dances in his rites.

PENTHEUS:

Asia's far less intelligent than Greece.

DIONYSUS:

In this, rather more. Our ways are different.

PENTHEUS:

You do these rituals by night or day?

DIONYSUS:

Night, mostly. Darkness has a solemnity.

PENTHEUS:

And guile, and rot, when women are involved.

DIONYSUS:

Debauch can be contrived as well by day.

PENTHEUS:

You shall be punished for your sophistries.

DIONYSUS:

You, for your ignorance and impiety.

PENTHEUS:

How pert a mystic! He spars, at least in words!

DIONYSUS:

Tell me my sentence! *What* will you do to me?

PENTHEUS:

First, I'll cut off those ringlets that you wear.

(CHORUS *begins drumming*.)

DIONYSUS:

These locks are sacred! I grow them for the god!

PENTHEUS:

And now surrender that thyrsus from your hand.

DIONYSUS:

You'll have to *take* it. I carry the god's own staff.

PENTHEUS:

Your person we shall guard indoors, in bonds.

DIONYSUS:

The god himself will release me, when I wish.

PENTHEUS:

Yes—when your Bacchae rally round you in force!

(GUARDS *outface* CHORUS.)

DIONYSUS:

Even now he is here and sees what I endure.

PENTHEUS:

Just where ? To *my* eyes he's not evident.

DIONYSUS:

Right here with me. Unbelief makes you blind.

PENTHEUS:

Seize him! This man is taunting me, and Thebes!

DIONYSUS:

Don't bind me, I tell you! *You* need control, not I!

PENTHEUS:

I tell you, bind him!—I have more power than you.

(*They do not bind him.*)

DIONYSUS:

You don't know your own life, your acts, or who you are!

PENTHEUS:

I am Pentheus, Agave's and Echion's son!

DIONYSUS:

An ominous name! Indeed you shall repent!

PENTHEUS:

Off with you!—Shut him in my stables there!

There let him have his visions—of gloomy dark!
There do your dancing! And these women you bring
as your accomplices, either I'll sell
the lot of them to slavery, or I'll take
their hands from that thumping and pounding of the
   drum
and set them to the loom, as slaves of mine!

DIONYSUS:

I'm ready to go—for what may happen to me
is not what *may* not happen. But for this
outrage you'll pay amends to a god you say
does not exist, Dionysus. Wronging me,
you lead away to prison the god himself!
                    (*Exeunt.*)

CHORUS:

Hear us, O holy and undefiled,
Acheloüs' daughter,
Dircë, virginal water,
kindly, for once in your sacred springs,
honoring Zeus, you accepted his fetus-child,
when from the deathless lightning he snatched it out
safe, to his thigh, to be born again. Said he with a shout:
"Come, oh thou the Twice-Born!—child of impossible
   things!
Enter this masculine womb of mine! Thus do I show
Thebes a god Twice-Born! She will call you so!"
—Yet you reject me, Dircë the blessed, now, when I
   bring
thyrsus-carrying throngs to await your will!
Why do you spurn, seek to avoid me still?

Ah, but I swear by the clustering
grace of the vine Dionysus in kindness did once confer,
soon you shall quail, dealing with the Thunderer!

Ha!—how he rages, this earth-born thing,
Pentheus, true to his breeding:
dragon teeth were the seeding
first of Echion who sprang from earth,
siring this monster, inhuman and threatening,
pitted against the gods, as a giant is!
Soon he will bind us with cords, who are no chattels of
    his
but the Thunderer's own. Even our priest, of more
    worth,
he has already imprisoned, bound, hidden away
deep inside his house from the light of day!

    —Oh do you see this, lord Dionysus, offspring
        of Zeus?—
    see how those who profess your divinity
    struggle in gross toils of necessity,
    forcible toils you alone can loose!
    Come down Olympus, your golden thyrsus up-
        raised in wrath,
    quelling this man of blood in his arrogant path!

Where, Dionysus, oh where among Nysa's wilds that
    breed
beasts of the wild, where is it now you lead
by a thyrsus hordes of the Bacchae? Where
on Corycia's summits? along what glade?—

or perhaps in Olympus' deeply forested glens ?—for there
by the sound of his lyre once Orpheus made
those same trees forgather, and savage beasts, to attend the Muse.

O Pieria, fortunate land!
Dionysus reveres you and next will choose
you for his dances, soon, and his mysteries!
He will come, leading his Maenads in many a whirling band,
crossing the rapid streams of the Axios
and the Loidias, river lavish in lordly felicities
to mortal man, and they call it a generous
father, who fattens the plains for excellent horses
with fullness of waters in wide glittering courses.

DIONYSUS (*Offstage, in a loud, roaring, bullish, but exulting voice, not the voice of his person disguised as a priest, which is lighter and feminine*):
Ho—!
O Bacchae! Hear me! O Bacchae! Hear my call!
CHORUS:
Who is that ? / Who calls ? / From where ? / It's the sound of our god's voice
when he exults, bidding us all rejoice!
DIONYSUS:
Ho—! Ho—! Once more I call,
I, child of Zeus, of Semele!
CHORUS:
Oh! Oh! O master of all,

27

master, oh come, stay
here with your celebrants, Thunderer!

DIONYSUS:

Goddess of Earthquake! Shake, shake
the earth to its base!

CHORUS:

Ah! Ah! The palace— /
Pentheus' palace, rocking in place,
will shake, shake /
till it falls! /
Dionysus is in those halls! /
Tremble before him! / I tremble, yes! /
See the stone lintels, over the columns, starting
   asunder! /
I see them! / Oh! / Our lord of the thunder
roars for joy of revenge in there!

DIONYSUS:

Catch up the thunder, the blaze of the lightning!
Burn up the palace of Pentheus! Burn! Consume!

CHORUS:

Ah! Ah! Look! Dare! Be dazed by the frightening
flame flaring there on Semele's untrodden tomb!/
Thunderstricken by Zeus, she left this eternal flare! /
Down to the ground, Maenads, tremble and fall
bodily safe to the ground! / See!—Pentheus' hall—
see!—by the child of Zeus is attacked, is burned,
is a devastation, is overturned!

(*Enter* DIONYSUS, *disguised still as the priest and with the lighter
voice, this time in a tone of great gaiety.*)

THIRD EPISODE

DIONYSUS:

Asian women, have you been so stunned, so overcome
with fear
down you fell and still you lie there? I daresay you must
have seen
how Dionysus sent an earthquake through the halls of
Pentheus?
Come, stand up. Take heart. Recover from the trem-
bling in your flesh.

CHORUS:

O to us the greatest, brightest light of sacred revelry!
Ah how I exult to see you, left abandoned and forlorn!

DIONYSUS:

Did it make you so despondent, seeing how they led me
off
guarded, into Pentheus' darkest dungeon headlong to
be flung?

CHORUS:

Yes—for what protector had I, if to *you* the worst befell?
But how *did* you get your freedom, fallen into unholy
hands?

DIONYSUS:

I myself, without an effort, easily made my own escape.

CHORUS:

Did he not even bind together both your hands with
running knots?

DIONYSUS:

There, indeed, I out-outraged him. He was binding *me*
—he thought—

yet he neither grasped nor touched me. Hope was all he
    fed upon.
What he found there at the mangers where he'd cast me
    was a bull.
On that beast he slung his nooses, round its knees and
    cloven hooves,
snorting furiously, from his body pouring off big drops
    of sweat,
setting fast his teeth and biting raw his lips, as I, near
    by,
sat down quietly and watched him. Just then Dionysus
    came,
making all the palace tremble; then upon his mother's
    tomb
lit the lightning. When he saw it, Pentheus thought he
    saw the main
palace blazing, so he started dashing hither and dashing
    yon,
calling to his slaves, "Bring water!" Every slave was put
    to work
laboring in vain at nothing. Pentheus let *that* struggle
    go,
as if meanwhile I'd escaped him; snatching up an iron
    sword,
back inside he rushed to find me, but this time the
    roaring god—
this is my opinion only, only how it seemed to me—
made a phantom out in the courtyard. Pentheus, charg-
    ing after *that*,
rushed and stabbed the gleaming ether, thinking he was
    slaughtering *me*.

More than this, the god of revels mauled him in still
    other ways:
wrecked his palace; now it lies in total ruin. Pentheus
    sees
now he made a bitter thing indeed of my imprison-
    ment!
Stunned, he dropped his sword and droops exhausted.
    Well, being only man,
he presumed to go to battle against the god. *I* quietly
stepped out here to see you, having little to fear from
    Pentheus.
But I think, hearing the thudding of a hunting boot
    inside,
he'll be out here presently—what *will* he say to all of
    this?
I shall bear with him most gently, storm and bluster as
    he will,
for to keep an even temper is the part a wise man plays.
(*Enter* PENTHEUS, *followed by* GUARDS.)
PENTHEUS:
    This is too much! That stranger has escaped
    when only now I had him forced into bonds!
    What! What!
    That is the man! How dare you appear out here
    before my very gates, once you got out?
DIONYSUS:
    Steady! Rein in your anger, to a quiet pace.
PENTHEUS:
    How did you slip your bonds and get out here?
DIONYSUS:
    I said someone would free me. Did you not hear?

PENTHEUS:

    What "someone"? You keep answering strangely still.

DIONYSUS:

    He makes the vine's full clusters grow for men.

PENTHEUS:

    [If so, his gift is madness to mankind.]*

DIONYSUS:

    To Dionysus, that reproach is praise.

PENTHEUS:

    [Where *is* the impostor, who assumes that name?]*

DIONYSUS:

    [Somewhere in town. But he'll be hard to catch.]*

PENTHEUS:

    I order all seven gates of the city locked!

DIONYSUS:

    What then? Gods take even battlements in stride.

(*Enter* HERDSMAN *from side.*)

PENTHEUS:

    Brilliant! What brilliance—and always misapplied!

DIONYSUS:

    I was *born* brilliant—where it most applies.

    But first hear that man's story, who has come

    in from the mountains with some news for you.

    We shall be waiting. We will not escape.

HERDSMAN:

    Pentheus, O master of this land of Thebes,

    I have come down from Mount Cithairon's peaks

    where falls of white snow never cease to shine—

PENTHEUS:

    What is there to make so much of in your news?

   * Interpolations by translator for probable lacunae.

HERDSMAN:

I have seen the maddened Bacchae, whose frenzy sped
their soft white limbs like javelins out of town,
and so I come, my lord, for the city's sake,
to tell you what terrific things they do,
greater than miracles. But might I know
whether I'd best recite my news from there
in full, or reef it in? I fear, my lord,
your great rapidity of mind, your quick
temper, and that extreme of kingliness.

PENTHEUS:

Speak. I give you entire impunity.
One must not take offense at the innocent,
but the more terrible the things you tell
about the Bacchae, the greater the punishment
to which I will subject the person who trained
our women for these disorders—this man here.

HERDSMAN:

A while ago, for pasture toward the heights
our droves of cattle were clambering over a crest
just as the sun began to cast its rays
warming the ground. Suddenly I could see
a host of women in three companies,
Autonoë heading the one, and Agave
the second, your own mother, and the third
company Ino. All were then asleep,
relaxed in body, some with their backs propped
against the tufted needles of the pines,
while others upon oak leaves on the ground
had carelessly cast their heads—but soberly,
not, as you say, drunk from the mixing-bowl

33

and from the sound of the flute, going to hunt
for love all over the woods and solitudes!
Your mother raised an echoing shriek, and stood
up in the midst of the Bacchae, bidding them
bestir their forms from sleep, when once the sound
of lowing from horned cattle reached her ears;
and tossing from their eyes the ripened sleep,
they lept straight up, in perfect ranks, a sight
beyond belief, the young wives and the old
and girls as yet unyoked. First they let down
their hair upon their shoulders and pulled up
their slipping fawnskins, those whose shoulder straps
had come undone, and belted the dappled skins
at the waist with serpents tamely licking their jaws.
Some, holding in their arms a fawn or the wild
cubs of the wolf, gave them while milk to suck,
all the young mothers with breasts still bursting full,
their babies left behind. They put on crowns
of ivy and oak and smilax in full flower.
One, taking a thyrsus, struck it against a rock,
from which a stream of pure cold water sprang.
Another drove her shaft into the ground
and there the god sent up a spring of wine.
And all who had a longing for white drink,
brushing the ground off with their fingertips,
had milk welling up in abundance. From their wands
with ivy trimmed sweet honey dripped in streams.
So that, if you had been there, seeing such things,
you would have greeted with prayer the very god
you now condemn. We herdsmen of cattle and sheep
gathered together, topping each other's tales

of what terrific things and wonderful
the women were doing. But one man, who had been
around the city and picked up city talk,
addressed us all: "O ye who dwell among
the solemn stretches of mountain, what do you say
we hunt Agave, Pentheus' mother, down
out of these revels, to oblige our lord?"
We agreed, and in the leaves of undergrowth
hid, lying in wait. They, at the appointed hour,
began to raise the thyrsus for the dance,
shouting with all their mouths the jubilant cry:
Iacchos!—calling the roaring child of Zeus.
And the whole mountain danced with them, the wild
animals danced, nothing remained unmoved
by the rush of women. First Agave ran
close by me. I lept out, to hold her fast,
leaving the ambush where I'd hid myself.
But she cried out: "O my swift coursing hounds!
These men are hunting us! But rally to me,
rally to me, armed each with a sacred wand!"
At this we fled, managing to escape
dismemberment by the Bacchae, but they attacked
our cattle that were grazing on fresh grass,
with not an axe in hand. You might have seen
one of them holding up in her two hands
a milk-fed bellowing calf, while others pulled
together, tearing heifers apart. Then ribs
or a cloven hoof you might have seen hurled high
and low—and things hanging besmeared with blood,
dripping beneath the pine-boughs. Violent bulls,
whose angered horns before were quick to charge,

were tripped and brought down bodily to the ground,
overcome by innumerable girlish hands.
They stripped the hides more quickly from the flesh
even than you could blink those kingly orbs.   (2.)
They went away then, lifted on their speed
like birds, across the plains below, which yield
by Asopus' streams abundant crops to Thebes,
and falling like foreign raiders on Hysiae
and Erythrae, villages inhabited
below Cithairon's rocky wilderness,
they overturned and pillaged all they found,
snatched babies from the houses, and everything
they loaded on their shoulders held in place
without being tied; nothing fell to the ground,
not even iron or bronze. Upon their heads
they carried fire, which did not burn their curls.
The men, being plundered, in anger took to arms,
and here, my lord, was the dreadful sight to see:
for javelins hurled by men did not draw blood,
but women, tossing wands out of their hands,
inflicted wounds—the women routing the men!
—not without one or another of the gods.
They returned as they had come, to the springs a god
had opened for them, washed their hands of blood,
while from their cheeks the serpents with quick
    tongues
licked off the drops, and polished fresh their skins.
And so, my lord, whoever that power may be,
receive him in our city, for he is great,
in all these ways, and also, I hear tell,
he gives to mortals the consoling vine;

take wine away, and there will be no love,
nor any other joy to mortals left.

(Exit.)

CHORUS:

I dread to speak the language of the free
before a king, and yet it shall be said:
Dionysus yields to none of the gods in power!

PENTHEUS:

Already too close, like a creeping fire, they catch,
these enormities of the Bacchae!—to the Greeks
an infamy! We must not hesitate.
March now, at once, to the Electran gate
facing the mountain. Give the order to all
the infantry that carry heavy shields
to muster there, and all the troops who mount
swift-footed horses, or run with lighter shields,
or pluck the strings of bows. We shall attack
the Bacchae in force! No, but it's far too much
if we endure from women what we endure!

DIONYSUS:

You do not listen, do you, to what I say,
Pentheus? Though badly treated at your hands,
I still advise you, not to take up arms
against a god, but stay here peaceably.
The roaring god will not stand by and see
his Bacchae flushed from those ecstatic hills!

PENTHEUS:

Stop telling me what to think! You escaped. Stay free,
or must I bring justice round on you again?

DIONYSUS:

I'd sacrifice to him, not rage and kick

37

against the pricks, a mortal against a god.

PENTHEUS:

I'll sacrifice: and such a slaughter of beasts—
females, for *this* god—I'll set Cithairon reeling.

DIONYSUS:

You will all be routed, shamefully, your shields
of bronze unable to face the Bacchae's wands.

PENTHEUS:

This stranger we grapple with is out of hand.
Dealt with or dealing, he must prattle on!

DIONYSUS:

But sir, all this can still be well arranged.

PENTHEUS:

If I do what? Take orders from my slaves?

DIONYSUS:

I'll bring the women back without armed force.

PENTHEUS:

Not this! Now he contrives a trap for me!

DIONYSUS:

No trap. I want to save you by my arts.

PENTHEUS:

You're all in league, to perpetuate these rites!

DIONYSUS:

I *am* in league for that—but with the god.

PENTHEUS:

Bring out my weapons!—No more talk from you!

DIONYSUS:

Wait!
Do you want to observe their council in the hills?

PENTHEUS:

Indeed I do! I'd pay vast weights of gold!

DIONYSUS:

What? Has so great a yearning come over you?

PENTHEUS:

Though it must gall me to see them sodden drunk—

DIONYSUS:

Still you'd be pleased to see what brings you pain?

PENTHEUS:

In silence, though—posted under the pines.

DIONYSUS:

They'll trace you out, though you come stealthily.

PENTHEUS:

Openly then. That much you have made plain.

DIONYSUS:

Then shall I guide you? Are you ready to start?

PENTHEUS:

Guide me at once. I even resent delay.

DIONYSUS:

First you must swathe yourself in a linen gown.

PENTHEUS:

What now? Must I rank with women, no longer man?

DIONYSUS:

They'll kill you, once they spot you as a man.

PENTHEUS:

Again well said. You're an old hand at this.

DIONYSUS:

Dionysus was my master in these arts.

PENTHEUS:

Then how do we carry out what you propose?

DIONYSUS:

I'll come inside the palace and dress you up.

PENTHEUS:

    What dress ? A woman's ? No, I am ashamed.

DIONYSUS:

    You're not so eager to watch the Bacchae now ?

PENTHEUS:

    What costume is it you say I must put on ?

DIONYSUS:

    First, on your head a long and flowing wig.

PENTHEUS:

    And what will be my second embellishment ?

DIONYSUS:

    A full-length gown. A turban about your head.

PENTHEUS:

    Besides all that, what will you deck me with ?

DIONYSUS:

    A thyrsus, of course. A dappled fawnskin, too.

PENTHEUS:

    No, I could not get into a woman's dress.

DIONYSUS:

    In open battle you stand to lose your life.

PENTHEUS:

    Right. I must first go out on reconnaissance.

DIONYSUS:

    Wiser indeed than fighting loss with loss.

PENTHEUS:

    Yes—but—how can I pass unseen through Thebes ?

DIONYSUS:

    We go through deserted streets. I'll be your guide.

PENTHEUS:

    Anything—so they do not laugh at me.

DIONYSUS:

If you like, we'll go inside to make our plans.

PENTHEUS:

Why not ? I have prepared for all events.
I'm ready to go. Either I march in arms,
or I may listen to these schemes of yours.

(Exit.)

DIONYSUS:

Women, our man stands now within the cast
of our nets. He'll reach the Bacchae, there to die
and pay the price. This work falls now to you,
Dionysus, and you are not far away.
Let us punish him. First put him out of his mind;
inspire a nimble madness in him instead,
for with his wits about him he'd never be
willing to put on woman's dress, but driving
beyond the track of reason, he'll put it on.
I want to make him as laughable to Thebes,
led in a feminine guise all through the town,
as he was awesome with his threats before!
But now I go to put on Pentheus
the very finery he will take with him
on his departure for the underworld,
at his own mother's hand slaughtered and felled.
He shall discover Dionysus *is*
the son of Zeus, and born extremely a god,
the deadliest, as the kindliest, to man!

(Exit.)

CHORUS:

Soon—how soon ?—in the night-long dances
will I step with white, with white bare feet,

41

ecstatic, turning my throat high up to greet
the dew-drenched air, as a light fawn prances
in greenest pleasures of pasture, after she gets
free of the fright of the hunt, no longer surrounded,
at a bound clear of the tightly knotted nets,
and the call of the huntsman to rally the hounds has
    sounded,
setting them·on at a faster pace,
and she with labored gait and with bursts of speed
dashes beyond them, beyond the race,
safe to the riverside's level mead,
rejoicing in man-free solitudes,
in shadow cast by the leafy woods.

> What can our wits contrive, or what more glorious
> gift can come from the gods to men than a high hand
> over the foe, heavily held, fully victorious?
> Glory's the thing men cherish, ever, and in every
>   land!

Scarcely stirring, yet ever unerring
is the might of heaven, to have redress
of men devoted to headstrong ruthlessness
and not to things of the gods, preferring
their own infatuate view. But lying in wait,
craftily muffling the tread of time with delaying,
are the gods!—hunting their enemy soon and late.
For it never is good to examine and pry, betraying
ancient tradition for vanity.
At small expense of thought you can come to know
this: that, whatever the gods may be,
theirs is the power. What long ago

was thought and made lawful, tried and true,
has struck root deep into Nature, too.

> What can our wits contrive, or what more glorious
> gift can come from the gods to men than a high
>   hand
> over the foe, heavily held, fully victorious?
> Glory's the thing men cherish, ever and in every land!

Happy the man who escapes the sea-swell,
reaching the port.
Happy the man of toils as well,
risen above them. Lives of a different sort
different men pursue, each by a different way,
leading to wealth or to power.
Many thousand hopes attend many thousand men.
Some go on to success; other again
fail or fall short,
missing the hour.
But the man who lives in immediate happiness
every day,
him above all, say I, the heavens bless.

FOURTH EPISODE

(*Enter* DIONYSUS.)

DIONYSUS:

You!—you so eager to see what you should not,
concerned for what is none of your concern,
come out before the palace—Pentheus! I say—
and let me have a look at you, attired
as woman, Maenad, Bacchant—to spy upon
your mother and her forces. You do look

43

like one of Cadmus' daughters, figure and all!

(*Enter* PENTHEUS.)

PENTHEUS:

Really! I seem to see two shining suns,
a doubled Thebes and twice her seven gates!
To me you seem a bull, taking the lead,
and on your head there has grown a pair of horns!
Were you once a beast? You've grown very bullish
    now.   (*3.*)

DIONYSUS:

The god, unfriendly before, companions us,
our ally; now you see what you *should* see.

PENTHEUS:

Well, how do I look? Do I stand as Ino stands,
or with Agave's bearing—my mother, you know?
                 (*Very queenly posture.*)

DIONYSUS:

I seem to look upon their very selves,
looking at you. But this curl's disarrayed,
removed from where I set it under your turban.

PENTHEUS:

My fault. Inside there, tossing it back and forth
as I danced in rapture, I shook it out of place.

DIONYSUS:

Never mind. I'll put it back, for it's my part
to play your hand-maid. But hold your head up
    straight!

PENTHEUS:

There! *You* adorn me. I'm *really* in your hands!

DIONYSUS:

Your girdle is loose. And just below the ankle

44

the pleats of your skirt are slack and don't hang
straight.

PENTHEUS:

So it seems to me, at least by my right foot,
but at *this* heel the skirt is neatly hung.

DIONYSUS (*as he arranges the hemline below the ankle*):

Perhaps you'll thank me awfully for this,
when you find the Bacchae modest after all.

PENTHEUS:

How must I hold the thyrsus, in my right hand
or this, to be taken for a Bacchant more?

DIONYSUS:

In your right hand, and raise it when you raise
your right foot. Good for you! How your mind has
changed!

PENTHEUS:

Could I not carry now on my own back
Cithairon's cliffs and glades, Bacchae and all?

DIONYSUS:

You could if you liked. Your mind was not robust
before, but now you have the mind you should.

PENTHEUS:

Shall we take crow-bars, or shall I with bare hands
wrench up those peaks, one shoulder to their base?

DIONYSUS (*wags finger at him*):

Don't *you* go wrecking the shrines of mountain-nymphs
and the temple of Pan, where his shrill pipes are kept.

PENTHEUS:

That was well said. One should not overcome
women by force. I'll hide among the pines.

DIONYSUS:

    You'll find you hide in hiding enough to hide
    from women run mad, and you a crafty spy.

PENTHEUS:

    Really, I see them—in the thickets like birds
    caught in the close entanglements of love!

DIONYSUS:

    Well, it's for that you go forth on patrol,
    and you may catch them—if you're not caught first.

PENTHEUS:

    Attend me through the very midst of Thebes,
    for I alone am the man to dare this deed!

DIONYSUS:

    You alone are at pains for the city—you alone.
    A triumph you deserve is in store for you.
    Come on with me. I'll guide you safely there.
    Another will bring you back.

PENTHEUS: My mother, I hope!

DIONYSUS:

    All men will stare at you . . .

PENTHEUS: That's why I go!

DIONYSUS:

    riding in triumph home . . .

PENTHEUS: My weakness is just that!

DIONYSUS:

    and in your mother's arms.

PENTHEUS: You'll force me above myself!

DIONYSUS:

    Well, yes, in a way . . .

PENTHEUS: But I'll deserve no less!

DIONYSUS:

What a really formidable man you are!
You will go through such formidable things
you'll win renown standing as high as heaven!
Stretch out your arms, Agave—your sisters, too,
daughters of Cadmus! I enter this young man
in a great contest. Mine shall be the prize,
mine and the Thundering god's. Then we shall see.

(*He goes out, followed by* PENTHEUS.)

CHORUS:

On! to the kill!—fleet hounds of the Spirit of Madness,
    race,
on, to the mountain! There is a rout in readiness,
led by the daughters of Cadmus. Stir them, sting to the
    chase,
after this man, crazed, dressed in woman's dress,
coming among the women possessed, to spy!
First his mother will sight him, prowling, peering about,
posted on some sheer cliff or a branch on high.
Then she will rally the Maenads, then she will shout:
"Who is this, so daring, to come to the mountain here,
here to our mountain, Bacchae, to spy and peer
into our secrets, the mountain-dance of the first
women of Thebes? What is his birth? He comes indeed
not from woman's blood, but a lioness might breed
such a brute, or of Libyan Gorgons the wildest one and
    worst!"

O Justice! Go, be manifest! Stalk him, drive
the sword you carry deep in his throat, clear through!

47

Slay the ungodly, ungoverned, unrighteous one, the
        true
    giant breed of Echion, not to be left alive!

He of unrighteous mind and of anger ungoverned
    against—
O Dionysus!—you, and your mother's worship and
    yours,
frantically scheming he takes the field, a will without
    sense,
trying through force to conquer what endures
ever unconquered!—Death will correct his mind!
Best, obeying the gods without reserve or delay,
bearing oneself no higher than humankind,
live out as griefless a life as any man may.
I do *not* much envy the intellect. I delight
rather to hunt these other, these great and bright
goods that lead on through a lifetime spendidly spent,
daily and far into the night, if one will cast
out all forms of law without Justice, thus at last
reaching purity, serving the gods, being fully reverent.

O Justice! Go, be manifest! Stalk him, drive
    the sword you carry deep in his throat, clear
        through!
Slay the ungodly, ungoverned, unrighteous one,
    the true
    giant breed of Echion, not to be left alive!

Appear, appear as a bull, or a serpent showing
    a hundred heads or a lion flaming like fire to the
        eye!
Go, Dionysus, hunt this hunter
    of Bacchae, stalk him as stealthily!

48

Go, destroy with a smiling face!
Smile on him sweetly, throwing
round him the fatal coil, so he trips, falls, goes
    under
the droves of Maenads in headlong race!

FIFTH EPISODE

(Enter MESSENGER *from side.)*

MESSENGER:

O house of Sidonian Cadmus, the old man
who sowed the giant crop of dragon's teeth
here in this land, how prosperous you were
once throughout Hellas! Now I mourn for you,
only a slave of yours, but all the same . . .

CHORUS:

What's wrong? From the Bacchae have you any news?

MESSENGER:

Pentheus is dead. The son of Echion is dead.

CHORUS:

    Lord of thunder, what a great god you appear now!

MESSENGER:

What? Why did you say *that*? Dare you rejoice,
woman, over my master's being dead?

CHORUS:

    I am an alien here and singing a foreign hymn of
      praise,
    for I cower in terror of chains no more!

MESSENGER:

Do you suppose that Thebes is so unmanned
[she cannot force you into reverence?]*

* Interpolation.

49

CHORUS:

>Dionysus, Dionysus it is,
>not Thebes, who governs me now!

MESSENGER:

>I cannot blame you, except that it is base
>rejoicing over misfortunes beyond cure.

CHORUS:

>Tell me the story, describe to me how he dies,
>the unrighteous man scheming unrighteousness!

MESSENGER:

>When we had passed the outermost farms of Thebes,
>fording Asopus' streams, we then set out
>into Cithairon's rocky wilderness,
>Pentheus and I—for I accompanied
>my master—and the stranger, who came with us
>to be our guide in reconnoitering.
>Then our first halt was in a grassy glen.
>We kept a soundlessness of foot and tongue,
>so we might see and not ourselves be seen.
>Below, was a gorge among tall cliffs, drenched through
>with waters, and shadowed over by dense pines;
>there the Maenads were sitting, their hands engaged
>in happy tasks, for some, their wands undone,
>were crowning them with crests of ivy again;
>others, like fillies uncaparisoned,
>were shrilling a Bacchic hymn, verse and response.
>But Pentheus—ah, poor man!—having no view
>of that feminine horde, said, "Stranger, where we stand
>my eyes cannot reach to those false priestesses,
>but at the cliff's edge, climbing a lofty pine,
>I might see properly their lewd pursuits."

Indeed I saw then how miraculous
the stranger was—for seizing the top branch
of a fir tree high in the sky he pulled it down
and down and down till it touched the very earth,
bent round like a bow, or as a curving wheel,
being cut to the line, is draggingly revolved.   *(4.)*
Just so the stranger, guiding it with his hands,
bent over that mountain timber to the ground,
no mortal act, and seated Pentheus
in the top branches, then let the tree rise straight
out of his hands, but smoothly, lest it throw
its horseman over its mane. Rising aloft
to the lofty ether, it stood, still holding safe
my master in the seat upon its back.
But instead of seeing the Maenads he was seen.
For a while he was not sighted, high as he was,
and the stranger had by this time disappeared,
but a voice come out of heaven—the voice, I think,
of Dionysus, calling aloud, "Women!
I present you the man who mocked at you and me,
and at my rituals. Now punish him!"
and with these orders suddenly there stood
a gleam of awesome fire in heaven and earth.
The sky was still; the wooded glens were still
in every leaf, and you could hear no cry
of animals. The women had not heard
that roaring clearly, but they stood straight up,
with staring eyes. He gave the command again.
And then, when Cadmus' daughters clearly heard
the command, they darted forth as swift as doves,
all running with an equal speed of foot—

his mother Agave, and her sisters too,
and all the Bacchae. Through the torrential glen
with its rugged rocks they sped, inspired by the god.
And when they saw my lord, perched in the pine,
first they hurled stones at him with all their might,
climbing onto the cliffside opposite,
and shot at him with branches of the pines.
And others threw the thyrsus into the air
at Pentheus, a pitiful target, but they missed,
for at a greater height than their zeal could reach
he sat, poor man, fixed in his helplessness.
At last they shattered branches from an oak
and tried to uproot the pine with wooden bars,
but when they came to no end of their toils
Agave said, "Stand in a circle round
the roots, O Maenads, and take hold of them,
so we may catch this climbing animal,
lest it divulge the dances of our god!"
They then set to the pine their countless hands
and wrenched it up out of the earth. Pentheus,
sitting high up, fell hurtling from that height
to the ground, with continual screams. He must have
    known
how near he was to death. His mother first,
being high priestess, now began the kill,
and rushed at him. Off from the wig he tore
the turban, so that recognizing him
Agave might not, to her sorrow, kill.
Caressing her cheek he said, "Mother, it's I,
Pentheus, your own child, I whom you bore
to Echion. Oh Mother, take pity on me—

do not, for the wrongs I've done, kill your own child!"
But she, spitting foam, rolling her eyes convulsed,
gone out of her right mind, was in the grip
of ecstasy, not listening to him.
She took hold of his left arm by the hand,
and, her foot braced upon the poor man's ribs,
wrenched out the shoulder, not by her own strength,
but on her hands the god conferred such ease.
Ino was finishing off the other side,
breaking his flesh, and Autonoë, the whole pack
of Bacchae were at him. A general howl arose,
he groaning as long as there was breath in him
and the women yelling victory, as one
carried off an arm, another carried his feet
still in their boots. His ribs were laid quite bare
in the dismemberment. With bloodied hands
each woman played ball with scraps of Pentheus' flesh.
His body lies dispersed, one part below
the rugged cliffs, another among the leafage
of the deep woods, no easy thing to find.
His mother somehow got into her hands
his battered head, and stuck it on the point
of her thyrsus, just as if she were carrying
down from Cithairon's crags a lion's head.
Leaving her Maenad sisters to their dance,
she comes away exulting in the dread
trophy she took, back to the walls of Thebes,
hailing her god as Master of the Hunt,
First in the Kill, the Winner—in whose name
indeed she carries off the crown of tears.
As for myself, I mean to go away

from this event, before Agave comes.
Prudence and awe before the acts of gods
are the highest conduct and, I think, most wise,
the best possession those who have it have.

(Exit.)

CHORUS:

Let us begin the dance, Dionysus' dance!
Let us begin the shout now of deliverance,
over the doom of Pentheus, him of the dragon's brood,
him who assumed the feminine dress,
carried an ivied wand by the god imbued
surely for him with a special deadliness,
down to the world below,
having as guide, to go
on to his doom, a bull!
Bacchae of Thebes, you have finished off a full
glorious victory song, with a dirge, with tears!
Splendid the contest won!
Splendid the winner appears,
casting her hands dripping with blood
proudly about her son!

For here I see to the palace hurrying home
Agave, Pentheus' mother, with eyes convulsed,
stark mad. Oh welcome her, let her celebrate
with us this victory of the god of joy!

(Enter AGAVE, *carrying the head of Pentheus with the wig still on it but disheveled. Her first line may be delivered off-stage.)*

AGAVE:

Bacchae from Asia—

CHORUS: Ah! We must hear! She calls!

AGAVE:

I bring from the mountainside
a fresh-cut curling crest to adorn our halls,
a rich and a glorious prize!   (5.)

CHORUS:

So I see! And we celebrate too; we share your pride!

AGAVE:

With never a net I bagged this noble child
of lions ranging over the wild,
as you can see with your own eyes!

CHORUS:

But where, oh where in the wilderness?

AGAVE:

Cithairon . . .

CHORUS: Cithairon felled—

AGAVE:

yes, gave him birth—and slew!   (6.)

CHORUS:

Who first was victorious?

AGAVE:

I was the one!
"Agave has first blood!" my companions yelled!

CHORUS:

And second, who?

AGAVE:

Of Cadmus' house—

CHORUS:

That high house!—

AGAVE: there were bred more huntresses—

but after me!—in third or second place—
who touched this game we won!

CHORUS:

Ah, what a glorious, a godly deed all three have done!

AGAVE:

Come to my banquet now!

CHORUS: Spare me!—to no such feast!

AGAVE:

The youngling is tender. Look—
beneath his fine soft mane there is just the least
beginning of beard on his chin!

CHORUS:

By the look of that mane it could be a beast she took!

AGAVE:

Our priest is a knowing hunter. Knowingly
he treed this beast, this trophy you see,
and set the Maenads on to win!

CHORUS:

Yes, for our god is a hunting god!

AGAVE:

You praise me?

CHORUS: I praise indeed!

AGAVE:

And soon the city will!

CHORUS:

And Pentheus, too, your son!

AGAVE:

Yes, when he knows
his mother took this game of the lion breed!

CHORUS:

Superb the kill!

AGAVE:

Superbly done!

CHORUS:

You rejoice?

AGAVE: I exult, ecstatically,

for I have wrought high things for all to see,
as this my trophy shows!

CHORUS:

Then show, poor woman, to the citizens
that trophy of your triumph you bring home!

SIXTH EPISODE

AGAVE:

You of this city with its noble towers,
people of Thebes, come and behold this prize,
the beast we daughters of Cadmus hunted down,
not with the strap-slung spears of Thessaly
nor hunting nets but with our soft white hands.
Where is your boasting now? What is the use
of buying gear from armorers, when I
with this my hand have caught such game as this,
and torn the joints of the beast all ways apart?
But where is my old father? Let him come.
And where is my son Pentheus? Let him get
a jointed ladder to mount the palace front
and on the high triglyphs nail this lion's head,
which I myself have hunted and brought home!

(*Enter* CADMUS *with several attendants bearing a litter with
Pentheus' body covered.*)

57

CADMUS:

    Come this way, carrying the ruined weight
of Pentheus, this way, servants, here before
the palace, him whose body I bring back
after innumerable search and toil,
finding it scattered through Cithairon's glades,
and nothing in one place, but everywhere
through the bewildering forest out of sight.
I heard from someone what my daughters dared
only when here in town, within the walls,
when I'd walked back with old Tiresias
from the dancing Bacchae. Then I turned my steps
again to the mountain, to reclaim my child
killed by the Maenads. And I found still there
Autonoë, Actaeon's mother once
by Aristaeus, and along with her
Ino, both raving mad in the oaken groves,
but someone said Agave, with a stride
of rapture, was upon her way back here.
And what I heard was true, for there she is,
and in my eyes far from a happy sight.

AGAVE:

    Father, if ever, now you can be proud:
you have bred by far the greatest daughters of all—
all of your daughters, I say, but most myself,
who, leaving behind the shuttles at the loom,
have come to greater things, to hunt wild beasts
with my bare hands. Here in my arms I bear
this noblest of our trophies, as you see,
to be set up against your palace front!
Accept it, father, from my hands; exult

in my good hunting. Call your friends to dine,
for you have come to fortune, fortune most high,
considering we have done such deeds as this!

CADMUS:

Immeasurable grief, such grief is more
than eyes can look upon. Sheer butchery
is what you have done with those pathetic hands!
What a fine sacrifice you give the gods,
and ask all Thebans here and me to dine!
Alas for your undoing, and my own!
And how this god, if justly, still to excess,
destroys us—a thundering god—born to our house!

AGAVE:

How crabbed old age is in man, and how
sourly it scowls at one! I wish my son
enjoyed the hunt, bred to his *mother's* ways,
and in the company of Theban boys
went after animals! But all he can fight
is gods! Oh, Father, it's high time that you
gave him a scolding. Someone call him here
to see in me the glory of success!

CADMUS:

Ah! No! My daughters!—when you realize
what you have done, how unendurable
the pains you must endure! Yet if, to the end,
you can remain as now you are, you'll seem
happy, not knowing your unhappiness.

AGAVE:

What's wrong with this? What reason have we for grief?

CADMUS:

First, turn your gaze away up toward the sky.

AGAVE:

There. Why did you propose I look up there?

CADMUS:

Is it the same? Or do you see some change?

AGAVE:

It seems more brilliant than before, more clear.

CADMUS:

Is that volatility still about your soul?

AGAVE:

I don't know what you mean—but I become
somehow collected. My mind is not the same.

CADMUS:

Now, could you listen, and answer, lucidly?

AGAVE:

Well—I've forgotten all we said before—

CADMUS:

· To whose house did you go as a young bride?

AGAVE:

Echion's, sprung from the dragon's teeth, they say.

CADMUS:

And in his house what son was born to him?

AGAVE:

Pentheus, a true son of his father and me.

CADMUS:

And now—what face are you holding in your arms?

AGAVE:

A lion's—or—so said the huntresses.

CADMUS:

Now look at it straight. It won't take long to look.

(*Removes the wig.*)

AGAVE:

Ah! What do I see ? What's this I'm carrying ?

CADMUS:

Stare at it closely, till it's clear to you.

AGAVE:

I see more agony than I can bear!

CADMUS:

Now does it look at all like a lion's head ?

AGAVE:

No. It is Pentheus' head—alas!—I hold.

CADMUS:

It has been mourned and mourned, before you knew.

AGAVE:

Who killed him ? How did he come into my hands ?

CADMUS:

Cruel truth—with what untimeliness you come!

AGAVE:

Say it!—my heart is bounding at what will come!

CADMUS:

You killed him. You and your sisters murdered him.

AGAVE:

Where did he die ? Somewhere at home ? Or where ?

CADMUS:

Where once the hounds tore our Actaeon apart.

AGAVE:

Cithairon! Why did this poor boy go there ?

CADMUS:

To flout the god and stop your revelries.

AGAVE:

But we—how ever did we land up there ?

CADMUS:

You had gone mad. The whole city was possessed.

AGAVE:

Dionysus has destroyed us. Now I know.

CADMUS:

You offended him. You said he was no god.

AGAVE:

Where, father, is the dear body of my son?

CADMUS:

Here. How I searched it out! I brought it home.

AGAVE:

Are all its members pieced together well?

CADMUS:

[No. And I did not find his head till now.]*

AGAVE:

[Dionysus must have placed it in my hands.]*

CADMUS:

[Yes, he reserved his best revenge for you.]*

AGAVE:

What part had Pentheus in my blind offense?

CADMUS:

He grew to be like you, and did not stand
in reverence of the god. But all of us
are felled in this one stroke—you—and this boy,
in whom our house is finally cut off—
and I, who, having no sons of my own,
must see, O my poor daughter! this last scion
of *your* womb horribly and ignobly dead!
Our house looked up to him—O child of mine,
                    (*Takes head.*)

* Interpolations.

62

you upheld my dynasty, child of my child!
You overawed the city. No one dared
outrage this old man, not before your face,
because you punished them as they deserved.
Now I shall be dishonored, from my house
driven into exile, I, Cadmus the Great,
who sowed the race of Thebes and harvested
a glorious crop! Oh, dearest of all men—
for even being no more you still shall be
numbered for me among my dearest—child!
No longer with your hand stroking this chin,
saying, "Grandfather," will you embrace me—child!—
or ask, "Who wrongs, who slights you, dear old man?
Who dares to trouble your heart with disrespect?
Tell me. I'll punish the man who does you wrong,
father of mine!"—Now, I'm disconsolate,
and you, his mother, pitiably undone;
undone as well your sisters. And if there be
a man whose intellect dare scorn the powers,
let him see this man's death, and admit the gods!

CHORUS:

Cadmus, I suffer with your suffering.
The justice that this child of your own child
suffers is well deserved, but harsh to you.

AGAVE:

O father, do you see how all I am
is overturned? * [how desolate I am,
who once was glorious, mother of the king
and a king's daughter? Now, what honor have I?

* Begins an interpolation to fill the "great lacuna."

What honor is mine to give, save to the dead,
my son, whom I must, with a mother's hands,
these hands that killed him, decently lay out
for burial—small solace for the dead!

CADMUS:

Touch him no further—he has been destroyed
by the god's anger. The body is accursed.
Until the Thunderer gives a clear command,
what hands in Thebes dare bury it? Its curse
might reach to the whole people, who can still,
being innocent, except for their king's guilt,
escape pollution, the god's height of wrath
which must, I think, be satisfied in *this*.

AGAVE:

What hands then will take care of you, my child?
Not even your mother's hands—if they were not
themselves polluted, separately cursed,
reserved, possessed, for actions of the god.
Can they do greater harm than they have done?

CADMUS:

I do not forbid it. If I should offend
the god in this, whatever pain he sends,
after this loss, will be no greater pain
and aged as I am, cannot last long.

AGAVE:

Who is this man whose corpse I hold in hand?
And how shall I, with even the greatest care,
gather him to my breast? What kind of dirge
am I to sing, to say farewell, to ask
pardon of every limb of yours, my child?
Under what mantles shall I hide those limbs

(SERVANTS *go fetch*.)

Come, dear old father, let us place that head
of this ill-fated boy where it belongs,
and let us fit, as exactly as we can,
the whole body together, shapely and straight,
so I may supplicate his head and each
and every part, adoring this flesh of his
that I once bore and raised so tenderly.
Oh dearest face, oh fresh young beardless cheek!
Here, with this veil I cover up your head.
Farewell! Forgive me! Of these limbs, blood-stained
and mangled, which one shall I mourn the most?
Why not this hand? Is it what I seized first?
How could I so have wrenched my own flesh apart?
So strong an arm! How perfect this body was!
His feet—so quick and firm in their kingly stride!—
still in their hunting boots. This much is well.
And these dead genitals, that had no time
to breed the princely future of our house!
Hand me those purple mantles you have brought.
I cover him thus, and thus I cover him.
Pentheus! My only son! Sleep well! Farewell!

CHORUS:

Will anyone who has looked upon this scene
deny Dionysus is the child of Zeus?

(*Lightning.* DIONYSUS, *in a bull-mask with serpents writhing about
its horns, appears on the battlement above the tomb of Semele.*)

DIONYSUS:

My people, of Thebes! Now you will know your god!

I show you my true form, and here above
my mother's tomb, in lightning, as I was born.

CHORUS:

The Thunderer! His voice! Fall down! Fall down!

DIONYSUS:

These people of Thebes, whom I so cherished once,
started dishonorable tales of me,
spreading the lie my father was some one
of mortal men. In their brute ignorance
they did me further outrage, who did them good.
I have destroyed your king, who wronged me most,
denied me, mocked me, cut my sacred locks,
seized my own thyrsus, and imprisoned me.
Therefore he is dead, and at those hands which least
of all hands should have killed him. That man there,
your king, has undergone what he deserved,
dismembered and dispersed among the rocks.
And what his people in turn shall undergo
I shall not hide from you. Soon they must leave
this stronghold, overrun by enemies,
led off as prisoners into slavery,
to many a city and through many woes,
until the gods consent to their return.
But you, Agave, never shall return
you and your sisters, exiled from this day.
I have brought them from Cithairon, to themselves,
back home to Thebes, only to say farewell.
You shall not see your fatherland again,
polluted as you are by a monstrous crime.
It is unholy that the murderers
ever come near the tombs of those they kill.

Go while you can, or else be stoned to death.
And into exile Cadmus too must go.
You told the truth, but used it like a lie,
to serve your interests and not your god.
Your hands are stained, but as you did not kill,
you shall remain three days to bury him,
your mortal grandson, building for him a tomb
which, like my mother's, no one must approach.
When that is done, old man, you shall not die,
but wander as a stranger in the world,
far east, far north, but never back to Thebes.
And when that ancient frame is overworn,]*
you'll change into a serpent; and your wife
Harmonia, daughter of Ares, god of war,
who married you, a mortal, shall be made
a beast, changing her form into a snake's.
You'll ride an ox-drawn chariot—so says
an oracle from Zeus—you and your wife
leading barbarians, with whose countless host
you shall sack many cities here in Greece,
but if they plunder Apollo's oracle
they'll have a desperate return of it.
But Ares will save you and Harmonia,
and to the land of the blessed bring you alive.
I, Dionysus, tell you what is true,
bred by no mortal father, but by Zeus.
Had you known wisdom, when you willfully
had none, you would be prosperous and blessed,
having won the son of Zeus for your ally.

* End of interpolation to fill the "great lacuna."

CADMUS:

Dionysus, we implore you! We did wrong.

DIONYSUS:

Too late. You should have known me earlier.

CADMUS:

We know now. But your vengeance goes too far.

DIONYSUS:

You outraged *me*—too far—who am a god.

CADMUS:

The gods should not, like men, give way to wrath.

DIONYSUS:

My father Zeus ordained this long ago.

AGAVE:

Alas! There is no appeal! We are cast out!

DIONYSUS:

Why then delay what is unalterable?

CADMUS:

My child, to what a miserable end
we all have come: you, your unfortunate
sisters, and I, unfortunate—so old
to go a stranger among barbarians!
And a still further destiny, to lead
a mixed barbarian army against Greece!
And then the daughter of the god of war,
my wife Harmonia, in a serpent form,
I, as a snake, must bring with me to lead
an army against Greek altars and Greek tombs!
Alas! I shall not rest from suffering!
Not even when I sail down Acheron,
down to the underworld, shall I have peace.

AGAVE:

I go to exile, father, bereft of you.

CADMUS:

Poor child, why cling to me, as the young swan
still clings to its old father, useless and gray?

AGAVE:

Where shall I turn, cast from my fatherland?

CADMUS:

I don't know, child. Your father is little help.

AGAVE:

Farewell, O palace halls! City, farewell!—
where I was born. In misery I leave,
a fugitive, who lived here as a bride!

CADMUS:

Daughter, go now to Aristaeus' house
[where Ino and Autonoë prepare
to go, like you, forever out of Thebes.]*

AGAVE:

Father, I grieve for you.

CADMUS: And I for you, my child.
And for your sisters also I have wept.

AGAVE:

This brutal onslaught Dionysus made
on all your children is a monstrous thing.

DIONYSUS:

And monstrous things I suffered at your hands,
my name not honored here in my own Thebes.

                    (*Exit.*)

AGAVE:

Father, farewell!

* Interpolation.

69

CADMUS:

Farewell, poor daughter—if you can fare well.

(*Goes into the palace with attendants carrying the body. A few* ATTENDANTS—*men or women—remain about* AGAVE.)

AGAVE:

Friends, take me where my sisters are,
the sad companions of my flight.
Let me fly far
and find a place
where stained Cithairon keeps not me in sight,
where I can see neither Cithairon's height
nor of the thyrsus any trace.
Let other Bacchae keep that holy rite!

(*She throws her thyrsus to the* CHORUS; *the leader catches it and holds it high. Exit* AGAVE. *The* CHORUS *addresses the audience.*)

CHORUS:

Many the forms of the divine.
Many an unforeseen event
comes on us by the gods' design.
We plan. They do not bring about
what we expect, and they find out
ways for the ends we never meant.
Such was the way this matter went.

(*Exeunt.*)

70

Notes on the Text, on the Translation, and for Production

The Greek text used is that of Paley, with much reference to the Oxford text by Murray and then Dodds. Many details of my interpretation were determined by Dodds' notes and commentary, whether in agreement or not. Many questions of meaning which, in this complex play, have to be left open by the scholar, have to be arbitrarily decided upon by the translator, especially if he is writing for the stage. Such decisions rarely mean I differ with Dodds on scholarly grounds. My indebtedness to him is also great for many a point of dramaturgy, but I have used little of his English wording, which is naturally for the British classroom and not the American stage. Diction aside, I depart from Dodds mainly in the coloration of the play, insofar as he is interested in anthropology and psychology. He makes much of the primitive rituals and irrationalities behind the play, and of the prurience in the character of Pentheus, while I make little, or no more than what seems explicit in the Greek. But wherever and in whatever I differ from Dodds it is without much assurance, if with some conviction and after no little deliberation.

Why another translation of *The Bacchae*? When several contemporary translations already exist, it is no longer a question of replacing nineteenth-century translations,—or that of Gilbert Murray, which is excellent, concealing in its English an incomparably rich and fine sense of the Greek, but impossibly dated because of its Swinburnese and other distractions of a period manner.

In our period several manners are tolerable and about equally contemporary. So are several views or senses of the very problematic original, though all of them will no doubt in time date as markedly as Murray's. My differing from the manner of William Arrowsmith and that of Minos Volanakis—the two contemporary translators with whose work I am familiar and to whom I am indebted for clarification to myself of my own manner or interpretation—is mainly due to discontent with their versification. It is free verse or "cadences"—which might represent the relative fluidity of Euripides or a more modern rhythm than a strict metric line but, to my ear, results in small, irresolute phrasing and gathers no impetus for passages of sustained eloquence to ride. Mr. Volanakis gets sometimes from cadence to jab, but this is an emergency measure, to recover some rhetorical emphasis from the dissolution of it in wandering cadences. All of which method is in or emerging from the tradition of Ezra Pound, which once had its great and clarifying use and now communicates with a very considerable public, but is a tradition with which, in spite of long acquaintance, I have nearly nothing to do. So far as translation of this play goes, Mr. Arrowsmith has got us ahead from Murray into a reasonably direct and, I believe, very stageable contemporary diction; and Mr. Volanakis, even with a rather rough command of English, has opened a way into a violent and pungent stage language—especially for the choruses—that has a validity of its own, and a beauty, though, as in the method of Pound, it uses the original very freely as raw material. I owe something to the accomplishments of these two gentlemen, though nothing in detail. My own accomplishment is by way of restoring a basic formality and a continuity of metric to the play, a consequent reinforcement of the rhetoric—not to say of what poetry may get into it—a bold but much needed filling out of the "great lacuna," several crucial matters of staging, and a closer approximation to what I gather was the late Euripidean mixture of styles. Still, I have underplayed a liturgical and archaizing vein which can be traced in some passages of the play. One makes much of it at the risk of sounding too distractingly like the King James Version.

METRIC

I shall not detain the reader with an essay, long, pedantic, and apologetic, on the metrics of this translation; but for actors who have to speak the lines and for the casually interested reader, I offer these rules of thumb.

The meter of the dialogue passages is a loosened iambic pentameter played against a good proportion of regular pentameters. (In "regular" I assume the traditional reversals of the iamb, the substitution of spondees, and elision, which are no longer heard as irregularities, least of all by a theatre public inured to Shakespeare festivals.) The loosening is mainly by introducing extra syllables, usually light ones, and this follows a license in the original known as "resolution," used by Euripides to a remarkable extent in this play, no doubt for speed, vivacity, and vehemence. My lines still contain the five conventional stresses of English pentameter, whatever the number of syllables to the line. The result could be considered a rudimentary kind of "sprung rhythm." For various reasons I have not tried to duplicate with English Alexandrines the Greek iambic trimeter.

The meters of the choric passages do not follow the Greek meters at all closely, for interminable reasons, but they gravitate to the choriambus (/ . . /) and to an ionic (. . / /) as do the choric meters of the original. The ionic was apparently the basic meter of Dionysiac dance and song. The beat of my choric verses can be followed pretty well, if one expects the choriambus or ionic at any moment, for my modulations from those feet are not great, only as far as what can be taken for the familiar iamb, trochee, anapaest, and dactyl. I do not involve myself regularly in such combinations as the pherecratic, glyconic, and so on, as the original does. Nor have I, to my knowledge, written a single dochmiac.

In one passage, after the collapse of the palace, I have used an approximation to the trochaic tetrameter or septenarius of the original: (/ . / . / . / . -/ . / . / . /). In a few of these verses the caesura has a comic emphasis, but next to nothing depends on observing it in production.

In the choruses I have used rhyme, sometimes in couplets or a / a / b / b /, sometimes more distanced or scattered. Since there is no rhyme in the original, and since most modern poetry does not rhyme or uses assonances, dissonances, or false rhymes, my use of rhymes, and mainly true ones, is not easily justified. And this is hardly the place to argue the advantages and the fatuities of rhyme in general; but in the case of Greek choruses, which were sung, rhyme does help the translation of them to be more a matter of sound than the spoken lines, more lyrical if you like and rhetorically more emphatic—differences which, with the loss of the music or in the absence of a new musical setting, can at least be indicated by the use of rhyme—in addition to more complicated rhythmical schemes than the iambics of the spoken lines.

I should add that the rhymes and the metrical schemes, even the simpler meter of the dialogue, lead to some distortions or elaboration of meaning, some padding and some *ripios*, but I have tried to keep these falsifications to a minimum. Many of them are exploited for emphasis, for point, and for clarity of sense on the stage.

STAGE NOTES

Though the following notes are not intended to help reconstruct the original production in 406 or so B.C., they do not depart radically from what that production may well have been. They are toward a modern—but not "modernistic" —production on a fairly large stage, with or without a proscenium, and with or without a separate area for a large chorus. Still, the choreographic possibilities of the play are such that a considerable dancing area, even if not so large as the ancient "orchestra," would be preferable to a shallow stage.

There are three main stage difficulties.

First, the set, which represents the front of the palace. Scholars have long worried about how the collapse of the palace is to be staged without absurdity, when after the collapse the characters go into the palace and come out of it and talk about it as if it were still intact. One solution is to treat the collapse as a halucination in the minds of the chorus. This solution is usually rejected, but not conclusively, and the possibility of conveying the collapse by a violent choreography for the chorus is enticing enough. Dodds thinks there may have been a token collapse, of part of the entablature. The language of the play indicates a more thorough collapse, and I do not think Euripides' audience, even if no sticklers for realism, would have been satisfied with so dinky a half-measure, and surely no audience but one quite cowed by the cultural prestige of the play and willing to put up with anything would put up with it now. I have another solution—without supposing I can be the first to think of it.

If the set represents the outer fortification walls and outer gate of the palace complex—which contains a large inner court and a number of buildings besides the main hall or *melathra*—it is possible to run this wall across the upstage and show *above* it the tops of columns and the entablature of the main hall, presumed to be well behind it. This upper part can fall out of sight during the collapse, with the effect of a whole, and be out of sight and mind for the rest of the play. Since Pentheus goes inside the palace after the collapse, and very probably servants go in later to get robes to cover the body, and most probably Cadmus and his attendants take the body in at the end, it would be as well to have the upper parts of other interior buildings appear above the fortification wall, right and left, as being the men's and women's apartments—which have not collapsed. I do not think the stables need be indicated, though they can be.

The set has a lesser problem, Semele's tomb. It is sometimes understood to be a construction in the middle of the orchestra, and a small version of the tholos temple of Vesta at Tivoli, with smoke emerging from the top, might be nice and not really in the way of the chorus. There is nothing much against this except the wording of the play which indicates a fenced-in shrine near the palace and perhaps a part of it. So I propose that the tomb be part of the architecture of the fortification, possibly replacing a part of it destroyed in the stroke of lightning that killed Semele before the time of the play. It seems to be elaborately screened by a grillwork of some sort with intertwining grapevines, and can be a rather tall decorative area against the grimmer stretches of the wall. In my interpolation for the "great lacuna" I have made Dionysus appear *above* the tomb. This is rather laying it on, but not a bad idea. If a director thinks otherwise, the lines indicating this epiphany *above* the tomb should be cut or rewritten. The possibility of showing the tomb inside the palace complex—where it really ought to be, since it was also Semele's bedroom—and visible by means of periaktoi or something, frankly I cannot think out. The top of it, with smoke emerging, could be shown above the fortification wall with the other buildings, but . . . .

The second stage problem is of the first importance. If the epiphany of Dionysus is to be an epiphany, and something of a climax, it can hardly be the mere figure of Dionysus disguised as a priest which we have seen since the prologue. His appearance in that disguise on the theologeion or in a machine in mid-air is a change but no epiphany to speak of, and a pretty feeble or anticlimatic switch. It is argued that the gentle smile of the mask of the priest is peculiarly horrible at this point, and I agree, but it is also merely vicious, even a shade cute. I think we need a larger, more unfamiliar, and more inhuman apparition at this very far-out moment. However, my main reason for proposing that Dionysus appear finally in a bull mask with serpents around the horns is that Euripides has built toward such an epiphany rather elaborately since the prologue. In reading the play, all the talk about his true form, the chorus' descriptions of him as a bull, and Pentheus' vision of him as bullish and with horns, are satisfactory enough as information about the real nature of the god, without demonstration to the eye—but not in the theatre. One cannot disappoint the *spectator* after so much preparation—except indeed for an even bigger and better effect than the expected one, which I cannot imagine.

In this connection it should be pointed out more clearly than usual that Dionysus has two distinct voices: that of the priest, light and even effeminate, and that of Bromius, the roaring god, which is heard during the collapse of the palace when the god calls from inside. (If the god's real voice and that of the priest were the same, the chorus would identify the voice of the god with that of the priest, or the priest with the god, when he comes out of the palace, and they do not.) The roaring or thundering voice may possibly be heard also at the end of the prologue, when Dionysus calls to the chorus off stage, and it certainly is during the final epiphany. It may be not a clear voice—as the voice of the god is not understood at first by the Bacchae, so says the messenger in his account of the death of Pentheus—and that may account for the repetition by Cadmus of what is to become of him, after the god has told him and us. The repetition may be due to senility, insistent lamentation, textual corruption, or emotionalization of the news by its effect on Cadmus, but perhaps also to the acoustic difficulties of the bass register. On the other hand, I have given the roaring voice a pretty intricate message, as I think Euripides must have, and it should be declaimed with as much clarity as possible.

A Greek actor, who had to take both male and female parts, would find the use of two registers, the lower one extreme, less of a stunt than a modern actor must.

The third stage problem is a matter of taste, but we are in the register of the macabre, and this bit of bad taste all too likely. When Pentheus is disguised as a woman he has on a long blond wig bound up in a turban. The Greek word for wig here is simply the unspecific komë—a head of hair. The word for turban is *mitra*, which does not mean the big oriental turban with which we are familiar, but seems to mean a simple wrapping to cover the hair, with which housewives are familiar. The word used in many translations— snood—is too full of the English Renaissance or *Vogue* magazine for comfort. Besides, a snood is frequently a net, and the *mitra* seems to be rather of solid cloth. Anyhow, Pentheus departs with his long komë carefully tucked into his *mitra*. The messenger tells us that when Pentheus is shaken down from the pine tree and faced with his raving mother, he tears the *mitra* from his komë. It is hard to bear, but I think this must mean he tears the *turban* off his *wig*, supposing his mother will now recognize him. Euripides makes no point of this in his narrative. It would be an especially cruel joke on Pentheus, and things are already bad enough. One may prefer to get around the whole business by translating the words "he tore off the headdress from his hair," or, "his snood *and wig* from his head," but this does not square with the Greek. I think Euripides slurs the point in his narrative —as we would say, does not milk the gag—because the main use of the wig, for direct shock, is to come later. As I am fully persuaded, Agave comes on stage carrying Pentheus' head with the wig still on it, disheveled so that it looks like

a lion's mane. The chorus says as much: That shock of hair
(phobë) does look like a wild beast's. Pentheus earlier wore
his hair short like an athlete—so we may infer from his
taunting of Dionysus for the latter's long ringlets—so he
cannot manage an adequately leonine look on Agave's entrance, without his wig.

The head of Pentheus is thus good for two shocks instead
of one, and for a more sustained interest. It is a sad fact of
theatre that, after its first moment of exhibition, the head
of the hero on a stick—e.g., Macbeth's—loses interest in a
matter of seconds, if something is not done about it. * The
head with the wig makes an unfamiliar and especially
fascinating Pentheus. But the wig has to be removed for the
scene which classical scholars refer to as the compositio membrorum—the reassembling of the corpse—in which the pathos
presumably has to be real and not fantastic. The moment of
the removal of the wig seems to come somewhere in the
course of Agave's horribly gradual recognition of the head for
what it is, as she gets back into her right mind, probably
just at Cadmus' line "Now look at it straight!" At that
point she seems to see the back of the head, and does not
really recognize it until after Cadmus turns it around,
saying stare at it closely. At this point the head is probably
turned away from us, toward her, and we "remember" the
face she now recognizes. This business, if not provably by

* Later, in my essay on the play at large, I shall propose that
Euripides introduced the feminine disguise of Pentheus into the
plot of an earlier play by Aeschylus. If, in that play, Pentheus had
no wig, this whole business would be a typical refinement by
Euripides on a simpler and broader effect in Aeschylus.

Euripides, is Euripidean. It works naturally on the stage and is harrowing, as well as a clever evasion of the frigidity of one direct exposition.

It may interest a director to know that in a production at Yankton College, South Dakota, the Agave, on full recognition of the head, clutched it with both hands to her breast instead of pushing it away in horror. The director, Kit Riker, was absolutely right about this in terms of modern theatre, so right that I think she must also have made an important discovery about the original handling of the scene. The desperate maternal gesture comes as a shock, but it is profoundly true and moving. It also prepares beautifully for the *compositio* proper, which does need some advance conditioning in the direction of pathos rather than horror, and, being so extremely physical itself, is best prepared by just this physical gesture.

NOTE ON THE "GREAT LACUNA"

Here, at the worst possible point in the drama, some fifty lines have been lost from the Greek manuscript. I think a good many more than fifty have been lost, considering the ground they had to cover; at any rate my interpolations, not so very redundant, would represent at least seventy-five lines of Greek.

They are in part invention, covering issues and motives that Professor Dodds thinks were probably covered and others that I think were covered by the lost Greek lines. Why does Cadmus not leave with Agave? How did Ino and Autonoë get back to town? Why is Cadmus exiled? Who will bury the hero? These questions are perhaps very small-minded, but Euripides was not the man to rise above them.

Interwoven with my inventions are translations of lines from the *Christus Patiens*, a Byzantine play pieced together from odd lines mainly from several plays by Euripides. A number of lines in that stupendously uninteresting piece of ingenuity were no doubt taken from this lost passage of *The Bacchae*. I have not had the stomach to search the *Christus Patiens* for more lines than those already indicated by Murray and Dodds. Nor have I listed which lines are mine and which are taken from the *Christus Patiens* or elsewhere. Only a specialist might be interested in such indications, and he should not need them.

Even the nonspecialist will suspect my two lines on Pentheus' genitals do not come from a Byzantine play about the Crucifixion. But the topic is both very natural in its place and traditional. Homer and Tyrtaeus at least do handsomely by the genitals of the dead. And here it is economical: its vividness obviates having to go into *all* the parts of Pentheus' anatomy, as Agave—on various evidence—seems to mean to do. It may still be too much for a modern audience, even if the whole *compositio membrorum* is not already too much, and a cautious director can cut the lines, considering the head, left arm, and two feet an adequate sampling.

PARTICULAR NOTES TO THE TEXT

1. *smilax*. I have never seen this plant, *milax* or *smilax* in Greek. It is often translated bryony, but I have never seen that plant either. The only plant with which I am familiar and which has, as smilax had, an evergreen leaf, white flowers, and red berries, is kinnikinnick, and that word is not Euripidean in tone but Aristophanic, like *torotorotoro-torotix* or *brekekekex*. So I do not translate. Smilax, pronounced

as if it were an English word, is sharper and rougher than bryony and I prefer its texture at this point.

2. *kingly orbs.* This wretched locution does not seem to be any better in the Greek and may well be worse. Euripides may be turning on a bit of Aeschylean elevation or just filling out a line, but so old a hand and so devious a mind cannot be trusted to be merely inept when he is not to our taste. It may be the messenger's notion of courtly diction, as his opening flourish was, and received with a like impatience by Pentheus. At the same time he speaks harshly of a fellow herdsman who has picked up city talk, and quotes his grotesque forensics. I don't know what to make of all this. The messenger can hardly be a comic, though he begins with a mildly comic moment and may have a few more such moments scattered through his speech, at the risk of spoiling its effect of terror and wonder. Perhaps he is an amiable sort of rustic, permitting himself democratic impertinences of a harmless sort under Pentheus' guarantee of impunity. I have to leave the problem of managing his tone to the director, who perhaps had best change *orbs* to *eyes*, and let it go at that. But in production the herdsman gives most of his long speech to the audience rather than to Pentheus, and this sudden reference to the king comes as a quite pleasant reminder in passing that we are listening not only to a very absorbing narrative but to a speech in a play. It is not the jolt you might suppose, but a sort of punctuation.

3. *bullish.* The horns of the god may now be visible to the audience. The later reference by the chorus to the bull guide should perhaps refer to something more striking and lively in the memory of the spectators than something only Pentheus can see. But if the reference is made in a spirit of

very savage mockery of Pentheus' "delusion" perhaps the revelation of the bull god to the audience can be completely reserved for the final epiphany—as I should prefer it. Still, Euripides is a demon for intermediate effects, and the horns appearing now would not seriously compromise the shock of the full mask at the epiphany. Oddly enough, the disguise of Pentheus too is incomplete. He still has his boots on, and the fuss over the hemline may be in part to show them, as a comic and sinister betrayal of his disguise. The Bacchae seem to be consistently barefoot. The mention of the boots later, during the dismemberment, is not likely to be an oversight by Euripides. The incomplete disguise—of Pentheus or Dionysus or both—would be a good example of clumsiness or imperfection used as a special grace, like a dissonance, and well within the Euripidean style.

4. *wheel.* It is not clear what is being done with this wheel in Euripides' imagination.

5. *a rich and a glorious prize!* I have insisted here on a secondary meaning of *makarios*—rich—to accommodate a fine story in Plutarch about the Roman general Crassus, who was rich on the imperial scale. When he was defeated by the Parthians in 53 B.C. his head was cut off and brought to the court of the king of Parthia. During the celebration it was carried by an actor dressed as Agave and singing these lines. Who would have thought the Parthians so civilized?

6. *gave him birth and slew.* This turn of irony is unaccountably not in Euripides.

"At Least the Most Tragic"
The Composition of *The Bacchae*

Whatever fault may be found with *The Bacchae*, it remains one of the most interesting plays in the world, and even a Sophoclean purist can want to know all about it. But early in coming to know anything about it one discovers it is, like the Bacchae themselves and their god, refractory to almost any kind of method. There is no inducing it to go along at all far with any theory of tragedy—Aristotelian or Nietzschean, arty or anguished. It goes against the historical development and decay of Greek tragedy, even against the other plays by Euripides. It will not readily behave itself on the stage. Its very climax, a uniquely atrocious one, is gone, with the loss of more than fifty lines from a Greek manuscript, and has to be imagined from clues among the ruins, like a pediment of the Parthenon.

The Bacchae is, if you like, composed largely of problems, many more than the above. And life, as the chorus itself pungently puts it, is short, so in impatience one may well be tempted to renounce theorizing altogether, to let the historical situation of the play go at the mere rough date of its first production, to consider the lacuna at the climax perhaps a mercy, and to read the rest, as it were, on a cash basis, for what one can get out of it by means of whatever modern responses one happens to have on one at the time. Unhappily, this direct empirical method is not much more satisfactory than the others, for the play is at times disconcertingly modern and at other times disconcertingly archaic. It will not stay remote and exotic like the Noh drama or Hindu plays and at the same time it really is not by Tennessee Williams. In places it is horrible beyond belief and in others unbelievably farcical and gay. Sometimes it seems to be simple-minded beyond endurance and sometimes so intricately subtle one imagines that Euripides, even as a contemporary of Socrates and the young Plato, must really have meant something simpler and is just warbling on. One can feel fairly sure that the descriptions of natural scenery were meant to be pretty, but just beyond this one spot of certainty, bewilderment closes in.

Along about here one's mental economics may demand a sheer shelving of the play; but if one has the time and the curiosity one may decide to start over, piecing together some sort of theory and a little of the surrounding history, reading up on other people's opinions, even recklessly restoring the lacuna, as I have done, in hopes of making a more continuous and coherent sense of The Bacchae, though not, in one's right mind, of exhausting all its problems.

Any reasonable theory of tragedy, if based on Greek tragedy, has to be somewhat elliptical, since not all or even many of the extant "tragedies" can be made to correspond to it; yet a tracing of their discrepancies makes their intrinsic features and qualities the more distinct, which is something and to the good. The discrepancies need not be taken for shortcomings or discourage attention. So the Poetics of Aristotle can still serve as a useful instrument of description for many aspects of any tragedy, even in the case of such an anomaly as The Bacchae, though what one can plausibly make of his theory is, as a ground of judgment, rather stultifying, and inadequate as well for describing either Greek tragedy at large or the range of significances one would like a general theory to take into account. The *Poetics* makes nothing whatever of *hybris*, of a "tragic sense of life," or of any evident "message" in tragedy, and one surely wants something of the sort, moral or philosophical, even if not too much of it.

Do be kind to Aristotle and any old theory, or new. It can have great value, in the exhilaration of abstract thought if you like abstract thought, in the comfort of at least partial description, and also in practical use, if it involves a set of rules of thumb for the writing of new tragedies. French classical theory, Unities and all, had a very uncertain foundation in Greek tragedy or anywhere else, but it was extremely useful to Corneille and Racine. And a more modern theory can be useful in writing more modern tragedies, however loosely it correspond to those of the past.

It was startling but entirely reasonable of Eugène Ionesco to claim Greek tragedy as a source. Not a little of Euripides does anticipate the theatre of the absurd. In turn, the theatre of the absurd clarifies many a moment of *The Bacchae*. Likewise the theatre of cruelty, under the theories of Antonin Artaud, may well claim *The Bacchae* as an ancestor and in turn make some of the emotions of the play seem less alien. Other qualities too, like its extreme physical theatricality and its minutely brilliant verbalistics, make *The Bacchae* seem especially congenial now. In describing it, one had best not forgo the resource of contemporary theories and intuitions, but include them with larger theories. Absurdity and cruelty are, if not essential aspects of Greek tragedy, common ingredients in it, and may not lightly be set aside in projecting a theory of tragedy in general. That of Nietzsche includes them specifically, though not as cardinal principles.

Aristotle, removed from *The Bacchae* by half a century, is a few millennia closer to it than we are, so in describing it I shall still make more use of the *Poetics* than of later theory. In projecting a few rudiments of a general theory also I shall prefer him, not as an authority but as rather less restricted by a particular epoch and a particular philosophy. As a man of the world and not of the theatre he has no special program of innovation for the theatre of his time, nor even of reform. The *Poetics* may not be as deep or intense as one would like, but it is broad. And it is far more a handbook of likely techniques for writing tragedies at any time, always worth checking over, than it is a set of criteria derived from such prohibitive categories as Being, Unity, God, Causality, and so on.

With his biologizing cast of mind Aristotle is interested not in what such a creature as tragedy means but in how it functions. For him its natural function is—quite observably—to give the audience a peculiar kind of pleasure, namely a mixture of pity and fear and other such feelings, "purged" of their painful elements.—Alas, I do not see that he means anything more profound by *katharsis* than that!—At any rate, producing a kind of pleasure and not edification is the special function of tragedy. Edification would be the special function of other kinds of animal, teachers and philosophers, apparently, and the kind of thought which tragedy typically and essentially uses occurs in the argumentations of the dialogue, revealing character and furthering the action but not improving the mind. Morals get into it, not as precept or example, but because the characters must be morally attractive or large enough for the audience to take them very seriously and be moved to pity and fear by what may or does happen to them.

Such a subordination or digestion of the philosophical and moral elements by the functioning aesthetic creature is no longer easy to allow. We may still speak well of the autonomy of the work of art, of pure aesthetic experience and so on, and we do speak contemptuously of the didactic, but at the same time our more serious theatre is thoroughly didactic. It is often overtly so, as in the plays of Brecht and Sartre, but more often in the guise of "protest." The protest may be philosophical, political, social, or even aesthetic as in the anti-art movement, but it is nearly all didactic and uses the work of art primarily as the vehicle of an idea. One may well worry about it, but one cannot reject didacticism in the theatre outright, perhaps because one enjoys feeling morally responsible, but certainly because in our time almost any idea of consequence has become not only polemical but violently dramatic, and can make exciting material for a play. Still, an essentially didactic play somehow does not quite make it, and why not? Should one try to have it both ways? Horace remarked that the writer who mixes the useful with the pleasurable has it made, and very great poets like Lucretius and Tasso thought as much. Still the relation of the pleasurable to the useful or vice versa remains a problem, and a very complex one in *The Bacchae*. Come what may, I shall start with Aristotle, for whom tragedy is a pleasure, period.

89

He says in passing that Euripides, for all his dubious "economy" of construction, turns out on the stage to be at least the most "tragic" of the poets. Whatever he may have meant by that, he should, logically, have meant that Euripides provided the greatest tragic pleasure, or pity and fear and the like in their highest degree. Not having the sensibilities of a fourth-century Greek as he did, and not having seen all of Greek tragedy on the stage, I do not feel that way about Euripides as a whole, but I do think *The Bacchae*, because of its extremes of pity and fear, must be the most "tragic" of his plays. If you agree with that, and take Aristotle's word for Euripides as a whole, you may think *The Bacchae* the most "tragic" of all Greek tragedies, and thus exemplary, even if for some reason you still think *Oedipus Rex* the "best."

Though Aristotle passes over the fact, Euripides abounds in ideas, both large and small. Aristophanes, in *The Frogs*, makes a great point of his excessive intellectualism. Nietzsche thought it was precisely the use of Socratic intellectualism by Euripides that at last brought on the "suicide" of Greek tragedy. In *The Bacchae* is a superabundance of small ideas but also of large ones, the drama turning mainly on the confrontation of serious rational man by an irrational, brutal, and playfully malicious divine power. The outcome, the insufferably cruel revenge of the god, has had various and uneasy interpretations. Once Euripides was thought to be making a final grand attack on the very existence of the gods, with his inveterate skepticism; or it seemed that in old age he must have recanted and abjectly resigned himself to the irrationality of Dionysus—too late, according to Nietzsche; now the play is thought nihilistic, or, short of that, a demonstration that the compassion of humans for each other remains a value, however appallingly the universe may behave. These ideas as such are not very interesting, but they are large; and if they or ideas like them are implicit in the play, Aristotle might say they were chosen for their size, or enlarged beyond the usual scale of Euripidean thinking, because they articulate the most universal issues, which can yield the greatest intensities of pity and fear. Euripides could write a domestic tragedy with a happy ending like the *Alcestis*, psychological dramas of great intricacy like the *Hippolytus*, literary tours de force or melodramas like the *Phoenissae*, and what I think are in the main *hilarotragoedia*, or hilarious tragedy, the *Helen* and the *Orestes*; but in *The Bacchae* the issues are ultimate or, if you can stand the word, cosmic—the relation of rational man to the irrational divine, reason itself to mysticism, the struggle of civilization against both barbarism and the natural powers, of the city against the wilderness, of the state against humanity, of the masculine against the feminine. It is these issues, their size and their inclusiveness—no one can feel himself exempt from them—that make the pity and the fear of the play so great. But again, I think Aristotle would insist that these issues are used not because Euripides as an intellectual had any novel or urgent ideas about them, but because, as an artist, he knew they would, when actualized and lived out on the stage, produce the maximum tragic pleasure.

The word "pleasure" may seem too slight for the ideological scale of *The Bacchae*, but it is a safe and sane generic term, dry, precise, and dapper in Aristotle's usual manner, and under the tragic species of pleasure may be included degrees like joy, elation, exultation, and so on. So with fear, which would include a range from suspense and apprehension to terror and horror. Pity has more degrees than our vocabulary distinguishes, going from concern, sympathy, commiseration, and compassion, to an anguish of "identification." All of these degrees—with a curious exception made of the "monstrous"—Aristotle seems to cover laconically enough in the phrase "such feelings." It is in the infinitesimal discrimination of all kinds and degrees of feelings and their mixture that Euripides excels, and I would call him by all odds the greatest emotional "colorist" of the tragic poets, but in *The Bacchae*, along with the subtlest variations of tone, he has a very powerful chiaroscuro of extremely bright and extremely dark feelings. The combination of archaic simplicity and already Hellenistic variability is, I think, what most baffles the reader of *The Bacchae* and makes a suicidal case of its translator.

Euripides had been a virtuoso of the pitiable as Aeschylus had been the great virtuoso of the fearful or terrific, even of the monstrous. Not that Euripides had never used the fearful or Aeschylus the pitiable, but it was Euripides notoriously who made the most and more of the range of pathos, including beggary and gynecological malaise. One of the saddest things about his Oedipus, blind and an outcast after all the concentrated catastrophes of the *Phoenissae*, is that he is now unemployable. But in *The Bacchae* Euripides reverts to terror of an Aeschylean scope or perhaps beyond, in fact re-working a play, the *Pentheus*, and motifs from several other plays on a parallel subject, by Aeschylus. I do not think this big square archaizing at the end of his life is a renunciation of his own style any more than the content of the play signifies a renunciation of his skepticism. The few facts we have about the circumstances under which the play was written may help to set this straight—and to account for the portentous apparition of Aeschylus, like a signature at the end of Greek tragedy, as he had been the overwhelming creative force at its beginning.

In 408 B.C., Euripides, then over seventy, left Athens to live at the court of the king of Macedonia. We do not know why, though there are many likely reasons—his relative lack of success as a dramatist in Athens, revulsion at the policies of Athens, horror at the long losing war with Sparta, money, a desire for tranquillity and perhaps for the adulation of a cultivated provincial court instead of the ridicule of the comic poets in Athens. Whatever his reasons may have been, exhaustion was not one. His comic verve was intact, his tragic gift may even have surpassed itself, his vivacity of analytic circling wit and his compulsive inventiveness were as acute as ever. In the less than two years before he died he wrote four plays. One was an *Archelaus*, about an ancestor of his host, the king. We know nothing much about that play, which has been lost, though we suppose it was produced in Macedonia. We know more about the other three—the *Iphigeneia at Aulis* and *The Bacchae,* which have come down to us, in however mutilated or corrupted a form, and an *Alcmaeon at Corinth*, which is lost but of which we have a fairly clear account by the late mythographer "Apollodorus." After the death of Euripides in 406 B.C. the three plays were brought back to Athens and produced. They won the first prize, probably on their merit as much as by courtesy to the great dead poet.

They were presented together, evidently as a trilogy, and may well have been written as such. A lifetime habit of writing in trilogies is not easily broken.

One often has to remind oneself that there were two kinds of trilogy or tetralogy in use from early in Greek tragedy—the consecutive and the assorted. One rather expects a trilogy to be consecutive, to begin with a wrong which brings a curse on a family and to follow the consequent disasters for three plays on end, for more or less three generations, going to show that the sins of the fathers are visited upon the children and the grandchildren. Not that the trilogy was invented to illustrate so questionable an idea; rather the idea served as a device for keeping three different plays causally together, and also made a wonderful ground for pity and terror. There is nothing like impending doom for keeping an audience with you indefinitely.

The *Oresteia* of Aeschylus more or less follows that scheme; so did his *Oedipodeia* and a lost trilogy concluding with the *Pentheus*. The *Prometheia* and the Danaid trilogy were consecutive, though not noticeably about a sequence of generations. But even Aeschylus used the alternate kind of trilogy, the assortment, a sequence of plays having no connection with each other except perhaps contrast or festive abundance. *The Persians* was written as part of a wildly varied tetralogy: the *Phineus*, *The Persians*, the *Glaukos Potnieus*, and a satyr play, the *Prometheus Lights the Fire*. *The Persians* is a reworking of a play by Phrynichus and so not an innovation but still a rarity in being a contemporary historical play about the battle of Salamis, in which most of the audience had been involved. In contrast, the *Phineus* was about a remote legend and, instead of the splendors of the Persian court, showed much physical misery long before Euripides made a specialty of it. It contained a spectacular and fantastic piece of showmanship, the Harpies being killed by the winged sons of the North Wind, no doubt swung about in the air by the notorious "machine." The *Glaukos Potnieus* was about a king whose mares ate a toxic vegetable, a sort of locoweed, went mad, tore their master apart, and presumably ate him. How that subject was managed we do not know. Were the mares, docile again after gorging themselves off-stage, trotted around the orchestra with the hero severally inside them? The satyr play, *Prometheus Lights the Fire*, involved the lovely conceit that a satyr, on first seeing fire, thinks it so beautiful it has to be kissed, but is warned he will singe his beard. Such seems to have been the extravagant variety of the assortment trilogy, or tetralogy.

In the consecutive trilogy as well, variety from play to play could be great and was probably expected. The only such trilogy to survive, the *Oresteia*, includes a heroic or public tragedy, the *Agamemnon*, a domestic or private tragedy, *The Libation-Bearers*, and a supernatural fantasy, *The Furies*. Its satyr play, the *Proteus*, is lost but seems to have been an animal comedy with a chorus of seals. Some of the possibilities, verbal and musical, have been charmingly worked by Paul Claudel and Darius Milhaud in their variation on the theme, *Protée*.

The chorus in particular changes violently from one play to the next—from Argive elders to Oriental slave women, to Furies, to seals. Or men, women, gods and monsters, then animals. The costuming and choreography of course changed with the chorus, but, more essentially still, so did the music. The need for a change to the more poignant or the softer

Oriental modes, Phrygian and Lydian at least, is probably behind the strange frequency of choruses made up of Orientals. Euripides in the *Phoenissae* is reduced to bringing a chorus of Oriental women into the Greek scene as tourists. Very likely the idea of *The Persians* first came to Phrynichus, more a composer than a dramatist, as a fine way of getting the Oriental modes into a Greek subject. The chorus of *The Libation-Bearers* is rather unreasonably Oriental—how did Agamemnon get slaves from eastern Persia or Parthia ?—but was no doubt accepted as a musical convention.

The chorus of *The Bacchae* motivates naturally a full debauch of Oriental modes, in various veins of religious ecstacy, lament, imprecation, longing, joy of revenge, and so on. Though the music is lost, one can trace the movements of its expression pretty well by the words, the way the topics go, governed mainly by musical considerations and not consecutive logic. Not that the text is simply a libretto or "book," but it is partly that, and I think a certain prejudice toward musicality and musical procedures governs much more than the choruses. Nietzsche seems to have had some intuition of this in writing *The Birth of Tragedy from the Spirit of Music*, but did not get down to the consequences of music for the Greek dramatic form. Unfortunately he had Richard Wagner more than Greek tragedy on his mind at the time. Short his authority, I still venture to think the subject of *The Bacchae* was chosen, both for its Oriental chorus and for its Aeschylean scope, to vary the interest of an assortment trilogy, a little as a modern composer might want a solemn and grandiose movement in a symphony otherwise given to quicker and more delicate feelings.

The *Iphigeneia at Aulis*—supposing it went with *The Bacchae* in a trilogy—is written distinctly in contrast to it. Its chorus is made up of Greek women, tourists who have come to look at the ships and troops gathered for the expedition against Troy. The chorus sings probably in nothing more outlandish than the Ionian mode. As usual in Euripides, it has almost nothing to do with the action, but provides lyrical and descriptive interludes. The chorus of *The Bacchae*, to the contrary, is deeply involved in the action and even embodies the major issue, as it had often done in Aeschylus. There are many other differences, but in general the *Iphigeneia* is a continuation of Euripides' earlier style, fluid, tentative, and nervous, in both the psychological and verbal motions, while *The Bacchae* is stabler and stiffer in form and its emotions are—with the exception of some pointedly volatile or *agitato* passages—more decisive and sustained. A minute but objective symptom of the difference in expression is the amount of *antilabê*, great in the *Iphigeneia*, very slight in *The Bacchae*. *Antilabê* is a change of speaker, once or more, in the midst of a single line of verse, giving a rapid and excited effect. The small but pointed use of it in *The Bacchae* counters the prevailing effect of one full verse to a speaker, which gives a stability and an Aeschylean solemnity to the stichomythy, or line-for-line exchange. The difference is something like that between a short staccato passage and a persistent legato.

The lost *Alcmaeon in Corinth* seems to have had still another style. Its mythological hero had already become a stock madman and matricide like Orestes, and might have provided an inversion of the theme of *The Bacchae*—son-kills-mother as against mother-kills-son—but it seems Euripides

avoided that rudimentary opposition and treated the Alcmaeon story as it were plagally or from a minor angle, a
moment in his wanderings when he recognizes a slave he has
bought as being his own daughter. The *Iphigeneia at Aulis* also
avoids a simple thematic inversion. Instead of the traditional
father-kills-daughter motif, we get Iphigeneia willingly
sacrificing herself for her country's cause. So there may be,
or there may not be, a thematic unity through the plays of an
assortment trilogy, and a deliberate variation from it. In
the *Alcmaeon* at any rate, the recognition of a lowly person as
of high parentage looks forward to the New Comedy of the
fourth century and later, or to the still later Greek romances
of piracy and long-lost heiresses. It is not typical of fifth-
century tragedy, though elements of the theme can be found
in Euripides' own *Ion*, or traced back as far as the *Odyssey*.
The reduction of the Alcmaeon story—which involved matricide, madness, and the war against Thebes—to a touching
episode is a distinct departure from high tragedy to family
romance, from heroic directness into a charming device of
Hellenistic art, the inclusion of a heroic theme inside a
trivial or decorative framework. The instances are very many:
the *Hecale* of Callimachus, the *Gnat* of Virgil . . . . The most
familiar is perhaps the epyllion of Catullus, where the
central heroic theme, the desertion of Ariadne by Theseus, is
reduced to a design embroidered on the draperies of a
wedding couch. It can very well seem that if Euripides, in
the *Iphigeneia at Aulis*, was continuing his own restlessly
analytic and psychologizing style, and in the *Alcmaeon*
deliberately reducing a standard tragic motif to decorative
romance, he figured that the theme to balance his trilogy, or
rather to point up the various delicacies of those two plays,

would be an archaic and superheroic one, after the *Pentheus* of Aeschylus. This would account for the peculiar stylistics of *The Bacchae* better than the supposition that he underwent a radical change of mind and style at the end of his life. We are not sure, of course, that the three plays were composed as a trilogy, but if they were composed at about the same time, *The Bacchae* is still composed in an alternate style, not a concluding one. The *Iphigeneia* looks much more like his last play, bearing many signs of having been left unfinished and then completed by his son as best he could manage.

The Bacchae itself is far from simply archaistic. Though in general it is more stiffly schematic and concentrated than the *Iphigeneia*, in detail it is extremely fluent. A statistical symptom of that is the "resolutions" of iambic feet (from two syllables into three), which occur at the very high rate of about one to every two lines. This license, in the midst of great strictness as to the integrity of the single line in stichomythy and the long, uninterrupted speeches by the messengers and others, is a good example of the mixed style of the play. But that style—the interruption and suffusion of the early structural style by the later coloristic style—can be made plainer in larger matters of the form. Let us follow, archaically, the questionable order of Aristotle, who lists the functioning parts of tragedy in descending importance as: plot, character, thought, verbal style, song, and spectacle.

The plot of *The Bacchae* is almost mortally "correct" in Aristotelian terms. It has a beginning, middle, and end, with no great deviation from the main causal course. It has a recognition scene (or two) which coincides with a reversal.

It even keeps to the three Unities, Aristotelian or not, of time, place, and action. If plot is the life of tragedy, as Aristotle said, this play is fully alive, a perfect vertebrate with an excellent circulation. Gilbert Murray called it the most "formal" of Greek tragedies, and its plot at least is one of the very tightest in the collection.

Years ago, after the break with Naturalism and the well-made play, it was generally felt that Aristotle was mistaken about plot, that it was only a perfunctory [routinely] convention for exhibiting the true life of tragedy, which was the felt philosophy of the author, or his poetry, or the inner life of the hero and a few other characters. For Aristotle the characters and whatever inner lives they may have exist only for the sake of the action, which can be determined and carried on only by characters making their choices and suffering the consequences. This point of view seems to me right enough by now, but the reasons are too mechanical. Aristotle seems to stop short at considering the plot a causal structure —a beginning leading to a middle which in turn leads to an end which leads to nothing more—underlying the other interests. But we have to consider even more rudimentary commonplaces than that to understand why plot is the life of tragedy, if it is.

Beginning with the brute facts of theatre, one may say a drama is a composition in a space of time. It shares this condition with music, as the Greek dramatists must have been perpetually aware, from the beginnings of tragedy in ritual, song and dance, and as long as the chorus was there to remind them. Before getting to a causal structure, one has the substantial existence of a space of time into which is introduced something in motion. The causal structure can be interrupted again and again by the chorus, but the under-lying continuity of motion in a space of time is not inter-rupted. The dancers were often in motion, the notes of the songs were of course in motion, and so were the words, whether sung or spoken. This primordial sense of motion is not peculiar to Greek drama, a result of its rather special origins; no later dramatist of consequence—least of all Shaw—loses sight of the words existing materially as motion within a space of time, or, if you like, in a temporal con-tinuum before they get to forming a structure of events or ideas. When we do get to drama proper, however episodically or consecutively the plot may be constructed, we have events in motion, the words are "in action," as Ionesco puts it, and on the stage the characters are frequently "doing some-thing," as Aristotle puts it, if only coming on or going off. Most important of all, for an Aristotelian, we have feelings or passions not merely in states but in motion. That is clearer perhaps in opera, but it is fundamental also in spoken drama.

These motions, their tempo, their changes, their flow or their abruptness, their intensification or fading, their modulation generally, are the primary articulations by the dramatist of his work in his basic material, the space of time. The word "rhythm" sounds a little precious in this connection, but rhythm of some sort, marked or inchoate, is as much an unavoidable form throughout the dramatic elements as it is in music.

For the distinct realization of motion there has to be a static or rigid element against (or toward or from) which the moving elements are seen or heard to move. In music this can be a key or a tonal center or metric or the continuity of a single voice or instrument. In the drama the rigid elements are especially plain in Aeschylus. It is said, I think rightly, that his plots do not move or change much, but are elaborations of static situations with only one or two big switches. The movement of the words, the music, the passions, is clarified and heightened by this. In regard to physical movement, his Prometheus is immobile on stage for almost the whole play, heightening the motions of the Oceanides in dance and song and the eccentric dance of Io, evidently, but also the movement of passion and the long recited accounts of the restless wanderings of Io. His famous silent characters—for example Clytemnestra on her first appearance or Cassandra for a long while after her entrance—give resonance and additional force to what is being said by others during their silence. This use of the static or blank for the realization of greater dynamics might be traced through all the elements, even character drawing, where the type character is often a better ground for emotional repercussion than the variable or developing character, and into questions of metric, where lines of one syllable can occur, with all the eloquence of the line of ten or twelve.

The plot itself is a rigid element against which the motions and passions can best be realized. The most varied passions, being made to move around a single issue or toward a single outcome, can seem to cohere with each other and strengthen each other. Singly, they gain strength by their extension into the future and out of the past of the plot, while still being contained within it, as they do not if they come at random moments or within an inconclusive field as they usually do in life. At least in the sense of heightening the emotions the plot is indeed the life of tragedy. But then there is the question, which seems to have been clear to Euripides especially, of how rigid or "inevitable" the plot should be, how slow or quick the sequence of events, how far the motion of the passions should be free to wander from the main issue. His famous "Euripidean" prologue, which sometimes not only describes the initial situation but gives in advance an account of the main action, is a very strange device, but no doubt meant in part to dispose of the rigid or structural element at once, so we can focus on the smaller and more delicate and wayward motions of the passions and other elements. The total shape of the action, during the time of the play proper, is indeed remembered, but does not clearly dominate what is at any moment going on. It is in dim focus as it were, a background, while the foreground details, relating to it perfunctorily and well enough to be contained, are highlighted in a life of their own more vivid than their relation "in perspective." In some plays, on the other hand, he keeps the plot changing so fast with unexpected switches that it is not really rigid in the sense of a reference point by which the audience have their bearings and their emotions can gain strength by duration until the *peripeteia*.

My friend Arch Kepner, who was not in Greek but involved rather deeply with American show biz and its jargon, gave me the best possible translation of *peripeteia*: the big switcheroo. The Greek word itself is most probably not philosophical at all but from the jargon of the Greek theatrical world.

The action-packed melodrama gives a series of instant emotions, sometimes of great intensity—thrills and shock and so on—and has a sort of rigidity in confining the feelings of the audience to the immediate present moment of theatrical time, what might be called a surface tension. It can be very exciting, but the excitement can be more of the nerves than of the emotions, and can result more quickly in fatigue and indifference. Melodrama is considered inferior to tragedy and perhaps it is inferior, but for practical purposes it is better considered another kind or tempo of tragic composition, and it is certainly true that the highest tragedy does not deny itself the resources of melodrama. Aeschylus in particular deals in situations so extreme they are nearly unbearable, and his uses of suspense and shock are intemperate, even if the rate of change in his situations is low. His *Pentheus* probably contained the most violently melodramatic recognition scene in all Greek tragedy, a scene reworked and modulated in *The Bacchae*, where Agave recognizes the head of her son.

The plot of *The Bacchae* is a combination of fast and slow, of rigid perspective and floating actuality. It begins with the patented Euripidean prologue, which ought to give us the story in advance but in fact does not divulge the major scenes and themes—the disguise of Pentheus as a woman and his murder by Agave. The mythological figure of Pentheus being torn apart by Maenads was probably well enough known to the audience, like that of Orpheus, from paintings, and even the scene of Agave with the head of Pentheus may well have been in the earlier play by Aeschylus and remembered; but the tragedians, especially Euripides, had been so much in the habit of giving new twists and effects to the old stories and plays that the audience could have had only the faintest idea of what to expect of this new version.

One of the reasons for the Euripidean prologue was

certainly that the main outlines of a new version, often at extreme variance with the old, as in the *Electra* or the *Phoenissae*, had to be set up at once to keep the audience from being constantly disoriented or bothered throughout the play by variations from other versions instead of accepting the main oddities at once and then attending to the actual drama, happily prepared, as it were, for any minor surprises to come. But the prologue of *The Bacchae* does not foredraw the main action. It is devoted to fairly succinct exposition of the previous action and the present situation, with virtually nothing said about the Pentheus and Agave story, except as it may be assumed in the threat of a forcible conversion of the city at large to the Dionysus cult. Much of the prologue is taken up with an insistence, necessary in a stage production, that the actual figure of the priest speaking is not the real figure of the god. He will, he says, reveal himself later—but the true figure is not yet described, and there would have been some suspense about whether he will appear as the bearded god familiar in pictures, as a bull, or a lion, or a many-headed serpent. It is in fact a very busy prologue, with a cunning use of suspense and the theatrical interest of disguise. It also goes in for the Aeschylean intoxication with large amounts of foreign geography, establishing both a breadth or elevation of tone for future reference and a sense of vast spaces beyond the stage which will support the later descriptions of the rituals on Mount Cithairon.

The prologue is a static scheme, compared to an opening with dialogue, but inside it there is a great deal of activity, and this is also true of the three messengers' speeches and the tirades by the characters. This composition in blocks, or long solid passages, as against dialogue interchange at a faster rate—up to rapid-fire and *antilabê*—is, one would suppose, not only archaic but undramatic and intolerably slow. It does not work that way in the theatre. I once thought it had to be left to the detailed vivacity of actors or reciters —as to the very polished vocal performers of the late fifth century—to keep these long speeches from total inertia, but in performance the play gathers bulk and weight by the protracted speeches, and the major dramatic movement is felt as a larger and larger movement, gathering and gathering as the play goes on. There is, even in the slowest passages, a sort of undertow.

The composer Normand Lockwood said of it, "For me it never stumbled, wavered, or let down at any point where it was, where it was coming from, or where it was going." The constancy of its movement or motion is clearer to a musician than to me, naturally, but still impressive enough.

The immediate movement inside the speeches is of course very lively just as narration and description—plenty is going on—but it is also worth noting that there is dialogue within the narrations. The messengers give direct quotations— sometimes indirect—from speeches of other characters— Dionysus, Agave, and an incidental shepherd. These characters are mimicked by the messengers, the result being a curious sort of dramatic sketch inside the narration. It is of course derived from the live recitation of dialogue in Homer, but within a play it is more than an extension of epic technique. It is especially effective in the case of Agave. Her voice and manner are mimicked twice by messengers and once by the chorus—as her posture and general appearance are mimicked visually by Pentheus when he comes on stage disguised as a woman—all this before she at last appears in person. In addition she is apostrophized by the priest long before she appears. These devices of presentation by indirection, by echo, reflection, or *imago*, have a remarkable future in Hellenistic and Roman art, especially Virgil, but that is another story and a very long one. It could begin with Aeschylus.

Back to the point: Agave is very much "prepared" and the preparation of the climatic figure contributes not a little to the onward movement of the play. This particular preparation moves toward a stage event, as the frequent mention of the bull form of Dionysus moves toward an epiphany of that form at the end of the play, and as the rather elaborate business about the wig and turban of Pentheus, on stage and off, prepares for the spectacle of his head on Agave's great entrance; so the onward *stage* movement is considerable, but the *dramatic* movement is also constantly furthered and made more expansive by the content of the long speeches and choruses, which, in spite of their high elaboration within themselves, are not self-contained blocks or showpieces merely, but drive ahead.

One may still have reservations about long messengers' speeches, especially as Aristotle says that tragedy does not use narration. His habit of defining things by their distinguishing features seems to exclude features shared by other things as well, but of course he knew that tragedy makes a considerable use of narration. Though narration is a distinguishing feature not of tragedy but of epic, it is in fact common to both, as is dialogue. Unreasonably enough, one still does feel that tragedy is not being quite itself when it indulges at length in indirect or narrated presentation of action instead of direct. But in *The Bacchae* that feeling is slight or lost, because the play of realities, direct and indirect, is already very complex; two of the characters are in disguise, two are hallucinated, and a general state of the unnatural and miraculous is on stage as well as off. The narrations, written moreover with extraordinary vividness, can seem as real as many of the things actually appearing on stage which are unreal.

In stricter terms of plot as Aristotle describes it, the play is—to adapt a term of his—"eusynoptic," or easily seen together, grasped as a whole. It does not go far beyond the slight "complexity" he recommends, a recognition coinciding with the *peripeteia*. Agave's recognition of the head as that of Pentheus and of herself as his murderess is indeed a switcheroo or reversal for her, but it also emphatically changes the center of interest toward the end of the play, from Dionysus and Pentheus to Agave, a "new" character. This device, of a sudden shift, with a new character, toward the end of a play, to keep it from lapsing into mere consequentiality, is already common in Aeschylus, as with the shift from Atossa to Xerxes in *The Persians* or from Agamemnon and Clytemnestra to Aegisthus in the *Agamemnon*. Of course in none of these cases is it a total surprise; it is implicit or carefully planted from the beginning. The device is worth studying, but not here, not beyond observing that the switcheroo of emotional focus is not used in that model of tragedy, the *Oedipus*; that it can be felt as a break in the plot, as when in the *Hippolytus* we go from preoccupation with Phaedra to preoccupation with Theseus and Hippolytus; but that in *The Bacchae* it causes no such feeling of disjunction, partly because the dead Pentheus is not only on stage and addressed lengthily by Agave and Cadmus, but is quoted by Cadmus and so has a sort of posthumous speaking part. If the emotional focus toward the end is double or more—Agave, Pentheus, Cadmus—it is not separated out in time and space but all right there at once, a trio of agony: the new character, an old one, and a much altered old one—*quantum mutatus*! Where Aeschylus, I think, tends "economically" to pace and space out his effects, even when he is laying it on pretty heavily as in *The Furies*, Euripides seems to be working his climax to a simultaneous multiplicity of effect, chordally as it were and no longer in a melodic style.

There is another and very curious complication of what were no doubt the simpler plots of the *Pentheus* and the *Lykourgeia* of Aeschylus. We know little about those earlier variants except that one or another seems to have contained a Dionysus disguised as an effeminate priest, the collapse of the palace, and a purely military or hunting expedition against the Bacchae. In Euripides' version, Pentheus is disguised as a woman and goes to spy on the Bacchae before possibly risking a military attack. Dodds in his commentary thinks the feminine disguise of Pentheus was a traditional motif and not added in by Euripides, though neither in literature nor in vase painting is there any sign of the motif before Euripides. It is coherent with anthropology, however, and the sexual ambiguity of the cult, so Dodds rather prefers to think it was not Euripides' invention. One cannot be certain, but I find it hard not to be, that the motif is indeed introduced into the Pentheus story by Euripides, and that it comes not from anthropology at all but from the *Thesmophoriazousai* of Aristophanes. That comedy, produced in 411 B.C., was a brilliant one, with Euripides himself as the main character. In order to spy on a council of women

planning the direst revenge for his detractions of the sex in
his tragedies, he induces his father-in-law to dress up as a
woman and infiltrate the council. The consequences and his
attempts at rescuing his father-in-law become a running
burlesque of several of his tragedies. It is not possible that
so recent a comedy, about himself, was forgotten by Euripides when writing *The Bacchae*, and I would say he obviously
lifted its main situation.

When Dionysus asks Pentheus if he wants to observe the
women in the hills he refers to them as *synkathemenas*, which
is usually understood to mean "huddled together" or
"seated together" or something suggesting an orgy—presumably Lesbian at this rate—but the word plainly means
"in conclave" or "in session together"—and could not, in
Euripides' mind or in that of his intended audience, fail to
suggest the council of women in the *Thesmophoriazousai*. The
scholarly problem is, by the scantness of evidence, not very
promising, except as it involves a theoretical one, the interrelation of comedy and tragedy and the range of parody.

What is known as "comic relief" was already familiar to
Aeschylus, used plainly in *The Libation-Bearers*, less plainly
perhaps in the chorus of the *Agamemnon*, but not so much for
"relief" as to disarm the audience for the full fresh impact
of the next tragic event or to draw off laughter in advance of a
dangerously hypertragic event, like the final encounter of
Orestes and Clytemnestra. Sophocles puts in some mildly
funny messengers. But such instances are not troublesome,
being episodes or intervals within a still very plainly tragic
play. It is when the comic is *blended* with the tragic that the
trouble starts. Even a comic parody of tragedy, as in many
scenes by Aristophanes, is not ordinarily a confusion, though

the tragic element makes the comic the funnier; and the mock-heroic is a distinct manner as early as the *Odyssey*. But a tragic parody of a comic theme, which we have in *The Bacchae*, is really troublesome, and furthermore rare before our time and the great use of it by Samuel Beckett. The most familiar older instance I can offer is the scene in *Lear* where Edgar plays a practical joke on the blind Gloucester, who thinks he is throwing himself over the cliffs of Dover but is on flat ground. Here we enter the realm of the macabre, or the hysterical, the sardonic, or the Absurd, a blend of the horrible and the farcical. Most of *The Bacchae* is well within this range, consisting as it does of practical jokes played on the hero by the god, some of them very funny but all the more horrifying. The very death of Pentheus, his being disguised as a woman at the top of a pine tree, and then, still with a dress on and a wig, confronting his raving mother with the announcement that he is her boy, may be Dionysus' idea of a joke, especially after listening to the fantasies of Aristophanes for decades on end, but it is certainly not our idea of even a sick joke when it comes. "Tragicomedy" is no word for this procedure now, though it should be the precise term, for comedy made tragic, not a mixture of tragedy and comedy. "Ambiguity" is no word either, since the compelling note is relentlessly and overridingly the tragic. From the sublime to the ridiculous is only a step, said Napoleon, but vice versa.

For theory, *The Bacchae* makes it plain that some uses of comedy, like some uses of melodrama, do not diminish tragedy or "relieve" it but indeed augment it (Ionesco says "underline" it). One has to insist on this idea, because theory tends to prefer integral kinds and peremptory

[handwritten margin note: unduly concerned w/ horror + death — ghostly]

exclusions—like narrative from tragedy and a tragedy that is homogeneously lugubrious throughout and a comedy that is undeviatingly a riot of laughs. *King Lear* and *The Bacchae* thus become oddities and exceptions instead of exemplary or resumptive tragedies—the most "tragic" of tragedies, as even a theorist may uneasily feel.

At the end of the *Symposium* Plato mentions a conversation about the comic know-how and the tragic know-how being the same. He does not go into the question, unhappily for us, but evidently the interrelation of tragedy and comedy was a distinct problem to the Greeks of the time, and Euripides may well have been experimenting with a special modulation of "tragicomedy" in *The Bacchae* as he had experimented with other modulations in the *Alcestis*, the *Helen*, and so on. The *Iphigeneia at Aulis* and the *Alcmaeon at Corinth*, as other modulations of the tragic "norm" into psychological melodrama and romance, may have heightened the effect of the hypertragic *Bacchae*, but also had a certain continuity or coherence with it by way of its lighter vein.

These idle speculations are hard to resist, for Euripides, not the deepest or best mind of antiquity, was certainly the most intricate and for us the most tantalizing. Was he being at all vindictive, witty, or dashingly experimental in combining Aristophanes with Aeschylus? If he did begin with such a clever idea, a gimmick good for a simple skit at most, like the first bare idea of the *Don Quixote*, it led him into much larger dimensions, as his bright idea led Cervantes, into a higher and more comprehensive tragedy from a comic base.

CHARACTER

The characters of *The Bacchae* are simple, overt types compared to those of the *Iphigeneia* or some in earlier plays by Euripides. It has been said that Pentheus is a stage tyrant, a sort of Herod, and it is hard to make him out a much more interesting case, even if you impute a subconscious to him. An actor can make him inwardly interesting, even a complex personality, by careful inflection of his lines, and Euripides may have written the part for a star actor in Athens to fill out with his special colors; but for a modern actor the interpretation of the part goes on very scant evidence.

A tragic hero, in Aristotelian theory, has to be "like ourselves"—not abnormally virtuous and effective, nor again inferior. He has to be capable of a mistake, whether or not that involves a "flaw" in his character. Pentheus is, like Oedipus, an efficient king and a man of direct action. In practical human terms there is nothing wrong with him; his mistakes are in dealing with the superhuman. He does rage and rave, and hot temper is perhaps a bad thing, as it is often supposed to be the flaw in Oedipus. But in the theatre, especially with an Athenian audience, excitable and irascible in the extreme, these angry scenes certainly draw sympathy. The rage of Oedipus against Creon and Tiresias may be morally dubious, but his suspicions of their intrigue against him are perfectly reasonable, the rage is justified; and for anyone in the audience who is not a moralist at the moment and has enjoyed at times getting into a rage, justified or not, Oedipus becomes intensely sympathetic.

I wish the word "sympathetic" could be enlarged to mean more than agreeable, and the word "sympathy" to involve more than the sadder feelings. It should mean, both as

Greek and as a dramaturgical term, *feeling together with*, even when the feelings are wicked, dangerous, or violently happy. For the moment I shall use it as if it meant all that.

So Pentheus is sympathetic, at least in his rage against Tiresias, since any Athenian at the time would have loved to wreck the oracle of Delphi—which had been against Athenian politics for most of the century—as thoroughly as Pentheus orders the shrine of Tiresias wrecked. And his rage against the Bacchae and their priest is, in a reasonable king, perfectly in order, and sympathetic, though dangerous, and so inspiring fear as well as sympathetic anger.

He provides one of the least ambiguous cases of *hybris* in all Greek tragedy. *Hybris* is primarily outrage, an act, before it is a moral quality or motive. It is often thought to mean overweening pride, and in moralizing about Greek tragedy this interpretation is comforting, since it introduces a familiar Christian feeling about pride as the root of all evil. However, pride is not essential in *hybris*, and though Pentheus, according to Tiresias, does have an undue pride of intellect, it is not specifically pride but a reckless devotion to reason, civic order, and clean living that motivates the outrages he does commit. His persecution of the Bacchae and his denial of the divinity of Dionysus are of course outrages, and so is his ordering of the shrine of Tiresias wrecked; but more: in the stage action his cutting of the sacred locks of Dionysus, taking his thyrsus from him, and leading him off to prison are very emphatically demonstrated outrage. This by itself may be morally satisfying, but is it anything more than didactic, a sort of Sunday school illustration or cautionary example? That much, even actualized on stage, does not make for pity and fear of any great

intensity. But if by *sympathy* the audience so to say partici-
pates in the outrage and at the same time knows the outcome or the full danger as the hero does not, then we have,
acutely, pity and fear. I think this happens in the case of
Pentheus, if his speeches are at first full of a charming
vivacity and his more and more violent rages infectious—
until the audience begins to feel he is going too far, or
rather, "we" are going too far—or worse, have already gone
too far. One may feel uneasy about the wrecking of the
shrine, but I think our full and distinct fear for him is
delayed until the actual cutting of the locks. Much of this
is up to the actor, since the bare text does not make the
progression clear, but the text does allow such a manipula-
tion, which is certainly necessary to the tragic effect as
understood by Aristotle. To repeat, as if it were a rule: the
audience must, by *sympathy*, be made to participate in the
hybris of the hero—up to a point.

There may be a good example of this method in the
Hippolytus. In the hero's long tirade against women, he
begins by entertaining us with a traditional topic. For
twenty lines or so he is delightful and the audience is with
him, but he goes on and on—outrageously—much farther
than a normal man or even a normal misogynist would go,
and we get into fear and pity. Aphrodite has probably been
listening to every word! The speech is more than a demonstration of character rendered with irrelevant wit, or it can
be more, and, for getting pity and fear into the audience,
had better be. Besides, the role of Hippolytus has otherwise
little appeal and must be played for whatever sympathy
it can gather in passing. Before resigning oneself to the
awful thought that Euripides in this speech is only indulging

his own view of women at inappropriate length, one should speculate—beyond the literal evidence—on what the most tragic of the poets may have been up to.

What with *hybris*, and what with pity and fear and being "like ourselves," Pentheus functions very well as the tragic hero. The chorus is against him, but since the chorus is up to no good, it does not necessarily set the audience against him. The Oriental chorus, rather like gypsies in later Europe, were probably understood on sight to be at least perfidious and most likely bloodthirsty and homicidal, as they were in *The Suppliants* and *The Libation-Bearers* of Aeschylus—all potential Medeas—so the audience's emotions about such a chorus were mixed, and, I think, kept mixed, as they are in *The Bacchae*. The chorus gains no credibility to speak of by being religious, for the Greeks had a strong distrust of any zealous sectarianism, especially Oriental, be it that of Orphism, Cybele, or St. Paul.

Pentheus is young, scarcely yet bearded, and that gives him a pathos, but does not make his actions particularly juvenile. He is, as Tiresias says and the chorus implies, an intellectual young man and highly articulate. In this, and in being physically very powerful, he is of the Hippolytus type, but not so complicated a mental case or a psychological study. Nor has he the deadly self-righteousness of Hippolytus. Mistaken or limited as he may be, there is nothing unsympathetic about him. I suspect there is a good deal in him of the Pentheus in the play by Aeschylus who may have been, as a young commander, not unlike the Eteocles of the *Seven Against Thebes*. However an Athenian actor may have been expected to enrich the part, I think it was meant as a simple and even traditional silhouette, affording an unambiguous ground for the vivid and varied motions of his passions, for the accelerandi and crescendi of his anger, but especially for the complications of his mad scene.

He has a special kind of madness—"nimble," or *elaphran*—in the late style of the author. It may be based on direct observation of madness, of the variable or "labile" state of mind, at least not on the convention of a fixed state of prophetic hallucination or obsession, as is mostly the case with the Cassandra and the Orestes of Aeschylus.

Even more to the point, the Spirit of Madness, *Lyssa*, only apostrophized in *The Bacchae*, was a real figure in a corresponding play by Aeschylus, one of his special grotesques like the Furies and Harpies. She is a good example of his tendency to spatialize, to the solid and the objective, as against the later Euripidean tendency to internalize, to volatilize, and to temporalize minutely, nearly down to the instant, as the "nimble" madness of Pentheus changes every two or three lines. He does not stay effeminate but swings off, as the Bacchae do when the spirit moves them, into a feeling of Herculean power, by which he can lift up mountains with his bare hands. He "sees things" both distant and close. And there are, within the scene, still other states of mind, even lucid moments, though their precise quality cannot now be fixed with certainty. Likewise the madness of his mother later on is variable, though less so, from violent exultation and queenly pride to light badinage and teasing.

The mad scenes have nothing to do with the psychology of the characters, however, the madness in both cases being induced by the god as unnatural states and not revealing anything repressed in a normal state—so far at least as the bare text indicates. With every opportunity, no such point is made. What an actor can, by accentuation and expression, make of the lines, and may have been intended to make of them, is another question. Certainly the intellectuality of Pentheus had to be conveyed by the manner of the actor, since nothing in his lines goes beyond an average knowingness. There is indeed more to him than meets the reader's eye, but how much?

One could interpret Pentheus as an oedipal case, with a latent effeminacy under the induced effeminacy, and a passive fixation on a quite exceptionally phallic mother. Euripides was capable of some such psychologizing, as the *Hippolytus* goes to show, but in *The Bacchae* it would be quite *Contrary* otiose to the action. In the *Hippolytus*, where the action turns on the fanatical and vindictive purity of the hero, some psychologizing is obligatory. The story of *The Bacchae* requires no such special case, and, I would say, for its full effect requires a quite normal hero, as "like ourselves" as possible under the circumstances. Pentheus is, apparently, fond of his mother, but not beyond the necessities of the overt action: if he resented her or were indifferent to her, or merely liked her, the horror of his death at her hands would be a good deal less. He is also fond of his grandfather, and anyone still interested in abnormal psychology can probably make something lurid of that, but nearly all of it has to be done between the lines.

And yet why restrict the potential of *The Bacchae* to what Euripides can have meant by it? A heavily Freudian or Jungian production might be very effective even now. Phallic symbols abound, if you care to read them, beginning with the thyrsus itself and then the ancestry of the hero, whose father sprang from the dragon's teeth and had the name of a snake (Echion). But one has to overlook the rather strange fact that in the play at least the Dionysiac rites have essentially nothing to do with sex. And one risks changing the whole play into a symbolical fantasy, when tragedy gets much of its power from the assumption that what goes on is practically and immediately real.

At any rate, in terms of 406 B.C., I think we have in Pentheus a relatively flat Aeschylean character—if the flatness is not from melodramas like the *Orestes*—as a contrasting ground for the vivid movements of various passions, their increase in intensity, their exhaustion, their changes and mixtures. These go on as events in stage time and do not accumulate into a rich and complicated or "rounded" character. The main characters carry the play—and the audience along with them—not by depth or psychological volume, but by power or force of feeling within their situations. In terms of modern theatre this is perhaps no difficulty, if character analysis and so on is largely out of fashion, but one had as well be explicit about it, since we may go back again to being deep.

Pentheus is more than the type of intellectual man pitted against the irrational, but not much more than a combination of that and the spirited young king. The characters are characterized, but very broadly, as they really have to be if they are to be grounds for full sympathy and not objects for curious study. The only character sketch done with quite distinctive details—the only "individual" so to say—is Tiresias. Euripides seems to have had it in for priests all his life, and this Tiresias is a remarkably sharp portrait of an ancient "Jesuit." He is full of modern science as well as of the most irrational dogmas, of shrewd political advice, verbal finesse, and grandiloquent noise. Being included in the general composition of emotional forces, he progresses from Bacchic rejuvenation to senile fatigue, just while the energy of Pentheus' anger, contrariwise, keeps increasing; but as a character he is more portrait than participant either in the scene or in the larger action. He helps to demonstrate Pentheus, as the object of his anger, and gives an added approach to the central issue of Dionysus' divinity, but as a satirical sketch he is objective and a good half outside of the intersubjective continuity of the play. That is to say, nobody except perhaps another priest can care how he feels or sympathize with him.

In his preface to *The Intent of the Artist*, * Augusto Centeno made a valuable distinction between the pervasive *intent* of a work and particular *intentions*, using as an example of intent Flaubert's relation to his novel, expressed in his remark "*Madame Bovary, c'est moi*," and as an example of intention, the figure of Homais. The life of Madame Bovary is, in the living, continuous with Flaubert's feeling and with the reader's feeling—indeed the other characters and even the landscapes, interiors, and weather in that novel are "lived" by Flaubert—everything except Homais, who is the object of a satirical "intention" and of very bitter feeling but is not felt from the inside. This is not because he is a villain—one can in all honesty feel with Rodolphe, with Edmund in *Lear*, and even with Iago—but because he is an object, a case considered only from the outside. Not that the outside cannot

* Princeton, 1941. Many notions and terms in the present essay come from the late Professor Centeno, in particular the prime importance of intersubjectivity.

be brilliantly rendered and more interesting than a living inside; it very often is.

It would be too much to say that every important character in a tragedy must be within our sympathies, even if one feels that way about it and Aristotle suggests as much in saying that tragedy is about people who are "worth while." Tiresias, as a partial break in the intersubjective continuum, need not be a mistake. In a play of such intense feeling one may welcome an "out," a sort of "objective" relief. The intersubjectivity of the theatre, like the single subjectivity, has to have its objects and may go so far as to treat a character as an object—falsely but with some malicious pleasure. Even in the *Iliad* there is Thersites, an object, described more concretely than any other figure.

Tiresias, as a very old man, is not altogether beyond our sympathies, or Athenian sympathies. Most of the young men were either dead or away at war, leaving a disproportionately elderly audience. That Cadmus at the end of the play is bereaved of his last heir must have been especially terrible to the audience of the time. That he and Tiresias are very old cronies was and is rather endearing. They are quite funny before Pentheus arrives, and that is a sure way to sympathy. When the old men leave at last, exhausted and trying to hold each other up, they are, after all, pathetic, and pathos is again an easy way to sympathy, besides being the great specialty of our poet.

Cadmus is an amiable scoundrel and no news for Greek tragedy. Homer's Odysseus had been largely such a type. So was the Danaus of Aeschylus; so was the Corinthian messenger in the *Oedipus*. Beyond unscrupulousness in the interest of his house, Cadmus has no individual traits to

complicate his major emotional ground—the great old
founding king. The messengers are differentiated—a guard, a
herdsman, a household slave—but their differences, beyond
a few verbal touches, do not color their narratives. They are
frames, not portraits. All told, the character-drawing in
the play has an Aeschylean breadth, overlaid by Euripidean
delicacies in the eventfulness of feeling, and all wonderfully
subservient to the main structure of action. I say wonderfully,
because Euripides gets consistently bad grades for psychologizing, lyricizing, and moralizing at random and at the
expense of his drama.

THOUGHT

Philosophical thought, like narration, is not an essential
characteristic of tragedy, but, like narration, it does get into
tragedy, sometimes in too large amounts for comfort. *The
Bacchae* contains, both implicitly and explicitly, even theological ideas. These go all the way to the final irrationalities.
The conclusive word of Dionysus, accounting for his dis-
proportionate revenge, is that his father Zeus ordained it
long ago. It is a horrible sophistry, accounting for nothing,
whether or not Euripides meant it to sound so, and the
perspective of the meanings of the world ends in a meaning-
less Predestination or perhaps Fate, with an arbitrary Will
of God somewhere behind it. This does not answer but it
disposes of the protest that gods should not give way to
wrath as men do. The gods do indulge in excessive revenge,
and that is that.

The Old and New Testaments have made that idea familiar, and the doctrine of the Trinity has made a multiple god
a familiar mystery. Dionysus is many aspects in a single

deity, but the play exploits two opposite aspects, both in extremes—his kindliness and his deadliness. Christianity does have the rudiments for this but ordinarily, being centered on the Crucifixion, does not make a production of the paradox that the infant or gentle Jesus and the Christ bringing a sword or the Christ of the Day of Wrath are substantially the same God. For practical purposes the Grace of God more or less solves that problem. One does not feel that the babe in the manger is a pretty sinister apparition, probably because it is not so much by his nature as by our fault in crucifying him that he turns out inhumanly vindictive in the end, even toward innocent bystanders like the unbaptized. But in Dionysus the double nature is vividly there, regardless of human behavior. His mild and festive aspect, worn in his disguise as a priest, is not only sinister but terrifying. He is the god equally of comedy and tragedy; here the two aspects seem to be superimposed rather than separate, or opposite like the two faces of Janus.

One could make a theological fuss about it, but one need not, certainly not here. For purposes of the drama one may say the theology is validated not only because it makes sense of the drama but because it corresponds to the double and unarguable nature of experience in the world, its pleasurable or festive elements and its horrible or catastrophic elements, which are not distributed very well according to what we think is human merit.

Whether such general ideas are taken at the theological or the worldly level, a drama containing them need not be a dramatization of them or a vehicle for them. Aristotle seems to make of them the material for the thinking that goes on in the dialogue, furthering the essential action of the

thoughts are spoke out in words of action

plot. The method for handling them, it follows, is that of men of action, statesmen, politicians, orators: the art of rhetoric. Ionesco, a superb rhetorician, speaks of words in action; he may mean as well ideas in action. But if the essential condition of drama is motion or movement in a temporal continuum, ideas can properly enter it otherwise than as factors in the causalities of plot, and in Greek tragedy they do. Among other possibilities, they can occur as events in themselves or as motion in themselves, as dance or song.

The most trivial idea, with little or no weight from a philosophical scheme, can, as an event, be vividly dramatic, not only in tragedy but in life as well. If you are traveling in a remote foreign country and unexpectedly run into a friend from home, you think and you have to say "It's a small world!" You may be embarrassed in saying it, but it is nevertheless a thrillingly real idea within the event, and its coming true is a wonder. Much thought in Greek tragedy is of this kind. The last chorus of the *Oedipus* says something to the effect that you cannot call a man completely fortunate until he is beyond misfortune, that is, dead. As an idea, abstract and uncommitted to an oppressively urgent instance, that is trite and obvious, but coming on the conclusion of the *Oedipus* it is devastatingly true, a sort of epiphany, and old as it may be, its occurrence is a raw event. Moreover, one cannot feel that Oedipus is a mere illustration of that truth, not when one is still full of the experience of his story, any more than one can, in the excitement of finding it a small world, feel that oneself and one's friend from home exist as a mere example of that rather frail truth. At the end of *The Bacchae* the solemn announcement by the chorus that the gods bring about things which you had not counted on is made at very "small expense of thought" if any, but as an event or occurrence in the temporal continuum of the play, and within the intersubjectivity of the theatre, still living the obsessive actuality of the story, it is apocalyptic.

So ideas, besides being factors in action, can be events in themselves and even make a sort of recognition scene with the audience as protagonist, but they can also exist simply as motion in the fundamental temporality of the theatre, in a lyric or choreographic mode. It is probably statistically true that most of the formulated general thought in Greek tragedy occurs in the choruses, which is strange, considering that with livelier meters and song and dance going on as well, the ideas are not as clearly projected as they would be in the spoken iambic dialogue. But for centuries epigrammatic and schematic thought, while it was a new discovery, had had for the Greeks an oracular and poetic intensity, almost requiring the accompaniment of dance and song. Sappho herself was a bit of a logician. Solon wrote political broadsides and Parmenides metaphysical essays in verse, not because prose was not yet a viable form, but because ideas, whether practical or speculative, had an excitement indistinguishable from the exaltation of poetry. Aristotle, to whom ideas had become prosaic—perhaps for the first time in history—makes the distinction; but the poetry of ideas went on and on at least until Lucretius, and some people feel it is alive in Dante.

According to Plato, Alcibiades felt in the discourse of Socrates an ecstasy as of flute music, so the contemporary choric disquisitions in Euripides may have had much the same quality and effect. Such a musicality would bring his ideas squarely within the intersubjectivity and livingness of

theatre, whatever their truth or importance objectively, outside the play. I would say that such ideas as one can take
home, not as memories of the play but as thoughts one can
apply in real life—didactic ideas—are simply fringe benefits,
and not the main purpose of tragic thought. Aristophanes
remarks that the audience should take home the thoughts of
the poets and put them away like quinces in their linens, to
smell of intelligence all the year through. Of course he was
a comedian, and comedy was far more didactic than tragedy
in the fifth century, containing a set lecture called a para-
basis and a formal debate called an agon, but tragedy too
could provide take-home ideas—*apophoreta*—that would keep.

As an example of a musicalized or choric idea which still
has a small portable content:

> Happy the man who escapes the sea-swell,
> reaching the port.
> Happy the man of toils as well,
> risen above them. Lives of a different sort
> different men pursue, each by a different way,
> leading to wealth or to power.
> Many thousand hopes attend many thousand men.
> Some go on to success; others again
> fail or fall short,
> missing the hour.
> But the man who lives in immediate happiness
> every day,
> him above all, say I, the heavens bless.

This passage, in translation fairly close to the content and
the motion of the original, is an elegant saraband of commonplaces, nothing one could call a contribution to philos-

ophy. But under its musicality is a very nice and useful thought for domestic consumption at odd hours: Though dangerous adventures and hard work can lead to pleasure once they are over, and people have many different notions of pleasure, whether or not they attain it, the everyday pleasures, if you are lucky enough to have them every day, are the best. The passage reduces in fact to a little hedonistic computation, to an aphorism from a graceful little ode.

But its real function is within the continuity of the play and within the longer chorus which it concludes. That chorus seems to be made of rather haphazard topics, but was surely arranged for a variety of musical effects, rhythmic and melodic, and the ideas serve largely as occasions for them. There are two hunting scenes, one a very pretty and lively one with a fawn leaping over the hunting nets, and the second more sinister and probably slower, with the gods as hunters slowly stalking the irreligious man. After each scene comes a rather bellicose and exultant refrain, probably much augmented in volume. After the second refrain comes the passage I have quoted, concluding the chorus with a tranquil and delicate and only moderately involved flourish. Since the music is lost, the interpretation of how the expression of the choruses went, their shifts and alternations and resolutions of mood, is sadly uncertain; but one can infer something from the mood of the verbal content and be reasonably sure the thought had, literally, a musical function.

The passage in question also elaborates the main issue of the play, though it hardly gets on with the action. Dionysus is of course the god of revelry, and one might suppose the range of emotion governed by that side of him would stay

musical function

pretty well fixed at the pitch of ecstatic joy; but Euripides, while keeping that pitch in his scale and striking it often, also develops the intermediate intensities and the slightest ones. The Dionysiac ranges, then, from ecstasy to casual amusement, from roaring joy to idly kidding around, and the corresponding ideas range from momentous to trivial, or "daily." Also his painful or tragic side ranges from wrecking palaces and dismembering heroes down to "work." Euripides seems to have had, as Aristophanes said he did, a democratizing tendency to the point of making everybody work, even at household chores like doing the laundry or fetching water. Whether his reasons were political, dramaturgical, or ultimately "musical," his inclusion of the minor issues, emotions, and ideas, while retaining, in this play at least, a full use of the major, is curiously Shakespearean. He maintains action at the Aeschylean level of heroic exploit, but includes a variety of chores. Even the Bacchae consider their wanderings all over Asia and into Greece not an exploit but work, though it is a "sweet" labor and they do it easily and rapidly. They have to repair their thrysoi, but that is a "happy" task (the deliberate mixture of pleasure and work is worth noting). Their exploits, aside from the traditional dismemberment of animals and heroes, are largely military—the plundering of villages in spite of armed resistance. That episode is probably left over from Aeschylus, but the interesting thing is that Euripides retains it as a dimension in this play.

Along with more splendid questions of value, there are several references to money, down to daily expenses and small change. Heroic wealth is of course in land, herds, and treasures of worked metal or fancy embroidery, but democratic wealth in the time of Euripides was in money and speculation. Pentheus threatens to *sell* the chorus off as slaves. Even in capitalistic societies, powerfully motivated by the romance of money or by bankruptcy as a definitive catastrophe, money is oddly felt to be well below the level of tragedy, unless it is referred to as gold. In nineteenth-century England, Fitzgerald can safely say "Take the cash and let the credit go" so long as it is really Omar Khayyam speaking with the exotic mentality of an Oriental bazaar. Our chorus says almost the same thing in business Greek. How the financial metaphors and suggestions in this play affected the audience in late-fifth-century Athens is hard to say, but Euripides probably meant them to be mildly amusing and distinctly unheroic, as a minor and intimate terminology of thought played against the monumental.

Monumentally speaking, the implicit and demonstrated "message" of the play is the idea expressed less fully and splendidly by Gloucester: "As flies to wanton boys are we to the gods. They kill us for their sport." *The Bacchae* does not mitigate that idea by occasional trifling, but augments it; the sport is not boyish but divine, or the next thing—Aristophanic.

VERBAL STYLE

The vocabulary is, for Greek tragedy, unusually rich, with archaisms abounding and neologisms of a rather tame kind as well. Unhappily, it is now impossible to tell exactly what these colors of vocabulary were, how vivid or how sustained, and what the affective content of them was. Some of the vocabulary seems to be "Aeschylean," but Aeschylus could also write in very basic Greek, so that in reading passages of the most "Euripidean" simplicity, close to the colloquial, one may be missing an Aeschylean ring.

Or a liturgical or mystical. But the religious tone cannot be that of the King James Version or the *Laudes Creaturarum* of St. Francis. The vocabulary often seems too simple for the occasion, as indeed so does "in the beginning" or *"sor acqua"* unless you belong to the same general religiosity as those texts. Intellectually one may observe they have a sublime simplicity, but feeling it is another matter. I can no more be sure of catching the exact intonation of many words and passages of *The Bacchae* than I can feel I am in tune with the Koran or the Book of Mormon. In translating the Greek word *adikos*, one has a choice of "unjust," "unfair," "unrighteous." I chose "unrighteous," as sounding biblical, and something remotely like that tone may be in *adikos* in a certain context, but I do not hear it. *Adikos* is normally a very simple secular word, ethical and not religious.

In this play especially there is a difficulty in appreciating a certain religious playfulness. One can tell oneself that Dionysus is the god of joy, of festive pleasures with wine and flowers, of quiet as well as violent revelry, but if one is still vaguely in the Puritan tradition as I am, one cannot feel that rejoicing in the Lord goes that far. The Catholic mind, with its frequent lightness, cuteness, and carnival spirit, is no doubt much closer to certain moods of the chorus than I can get. And I have only heard about the peculiar ecstatic gaiety of the Greek Orthodox Easter, which may well perpetuate something of the Dionysiac festival in the spring. I do like festivity and revelry and carnivals, but I cannot feel them as an integral part of religion. Some of the religious choruses are light in manner, very graceful and witty,

perhaps jocose, while others are as insanely fierce as the
Song of Deborah and still others have an incantatory
solemnity—or so one supposes from the content and the
rhetorical structure. One can only assume that Euripides
enlarged his usual vocabulary to meet a wider range of
tones and semitones of content than usual, and that the
words are equal to the occasions.

One can follow the grosser distinctions and the wider
intervals. The over-all theme of the play is not only solemn
but terrifying—a day of wrath and as Aeschylean as it can
be—but against this substantial and vast horror is played,
persistently, a gamut of pleasurable themes and tones. The
stridency begins with the grotesque festive exuberance of the
decrepit Cadmus and Tiresias. The exultant roar of Dionysus
during the destruction of the palace—a sort of divine
Schadenfreude augmented from the human *Schadenfreude* of
Pentheus toward the shrine of Tiresias—and the bantering
account by the priest of the baiting of the hero continue the
ambivalence of feeling. It exists, poignantly, in the mincing
gaiety of the mad Pentheus, but the climax of the effect is
the joy of Agave pitched to its utmost—her exultation in her
"trophy" from the hunt, in her imminent fame or glory, in
her pride as a queen of the house of Cadmus, in her superior-
ity to male hunters, in sheer physical expansiveness. Her
mood is as full and dazzling bright as Euripides can make
it, on the blackest possible occasion. It is a forced chiaroscuro of feeling, what I should call baroque, but it is over-
whelmingly effective.

In simpler dramatic terms it also negotiates a dangerous
situation very deftly: an audience might easily react to so
ghastly an entrance by nervous, or hysterical, or outright

laughter—but not when Agave herself is in a paroxysm of joy and doing the laughing herself. (In production it is not a bad idea to have her heard laughing off stage, on a rising scale, before her entrance.) Her joy, which might be repulsively maniacal by itself, is inflected toward the pitiable and subtly sustained by the vengeful rejoicing of the chorus and their baiting her. The number of minor tonalities within the brightest register of joy is astonishing, the work of a very great "colorist" and the father of the Hellenistic style. The effect is so compelling that the long laments after the recognition scene and even the *compositio membrorum* keep their dark and desperate effects unwaveringly—held firm, as it were, by their very strong opposite.

Such broad and powerful dynamics are both Aeschylean and baroque, but the finer distinctions and associations of tone are Euripidean and Hellenistic, or rococo. The fifth century gradually changed in its sense of beauty from the handsome to the graceful, though it was the fourth and later centuries that made a distinct speciality of grace, *charis*. This is plain in the history of sculpture, architecture, and vase-painting. The Nike temple on the Acropolis is a good example of dominant "grace" in both architecture and sculpture, and the very fluent or fluid calligraphy of late *lekythoi* or the painters "around Meidias" is already rococo. We are told Euripides was himself a painter; we might have guessed as much from the delicate pictorial compositions of the messengers' speeches in *The Bacchae*—as full of variable light and texture, elegantly distributed and graduated detail, calculated disorders and dimnesses, velocities and slow struggles as anything one can suppose about Hellenistic painting from the best of Pompeian. One cannot always make out a stylistic correspondence between the literary and the visual arts, but in this case it obtrudes itself. And in the fine art of morals and survival, which surely in part determines the other arts, the style in fashion was one of "grace" rather then rigor, fluent and approximate rather than peremptory. This is at issue in the *Hippolytus*, not only in the nurse's recommendations to Phaedra that she give up her arrogant and suicidal rigor for a more human flexibility, but in the chorus' wish:

Oh if my luck and the gods were to answer my prayer
    and my need
for wealth and success,
for a spirit unstained by distress,
keeping a not overstrict and yet not a counterfeit creed!
Had I a character easy to change
day to day to meet anything sudden or strange,
my life were one I might bless.

In the moral style we get thus a *disponibilité* and a variability in character to meet occasions—a style certainly created by dire practicalities in the late fifth century, as it was again in the late seventeenth, where it is the whole issue of Molière's *Le Misanthrope*. There is a corresponding style in the passions, as Phaedra's nurse declares:

Affection should be loosely fixed,
so one may have it tightly tied
or else unbind.

The looseness of attachment is also a pictorial style, where

the lines and colors do not bind or demarcate but flow
along or wander about and often float loose from each other;
also a musical style, the modes being distinguished as strict
or slack, and the Oriental modes, certainly worked hard in
The Bacchae, being the more slack or loose; and again a
syntactical style, where the connections are suspended or
imprecise, the progress of the clauses meanders and develops
subordination upon subordination, to fetch up on the plane
of simple declaration rather unexpectedly. We get much
hyperbaton, hyperbole, play with double meanings, studied
carelessness and inaccuracy—*où l'Indécis au Précis se joint*. It
is certainly a mistake, almost a serious one, to correct
"nothing in the same place" to "no two things in the same
place."

This is no place to take on a study of the Greek syntax, but
I say with intense feeling that the syntactical style of Euripides is extraordinarily supple and sinuous. In attempting to
follow it my translation may often seem tortuous instead,
but that is my fault and that of the uninflectedness of
English. At the same time, or against this fluid manner, he
can work a perfectly dry, flat, lapidary, or gnomic manner—
as in "Life is short"—various vocalizings or moralizings by
the chorus on incredibly commonplace ideas, abrupt asser-
tions by the characters, and the awful terseness of the final
ode, its last line dry as a bone.

The great Spanish art critic Eugenio d'Ors once applied
the term "emulsion" to the curious darknesses of Rem-
brandt—or of Goya—which hold, as it were, in suspension
many particles of light, quite a different thing from gray or
a simple intermediate tone. Some Pompeian paintings
manage this, and Hellenistic painting probably did. The

effect is plain in some Hellenistic pebble mosaics from Macedonia, if only by virtue of the medium. I can find no good instance closer to the time of Euripides than that— barring the invention of the Corinthian capital—but I would suggest that in *The Bacchae* the many graceful light touches, the small sparkles of wit, are suspended in the tragic mood in some such way. It is irony in particular which can keep up this minute or shimmering kind of chiaroscuro; the patter of the "bitter" Fool in *Lear* is a ready example of its use in the darkest tragedy. With a lighter ground one finds a sweeter wit playing through the comedies of Menander, a mixture of tears and laughter in a minor key. And it may mean something that Coleridge had an intuition of the "luminous mist" of Plato.

But as in the most atmospheric Pompeian painting there is often set the flattest and hardest-edged of silhouettes or an episode of unmodulated juxtaposition of extreme light and extreme dark, *The Bacchae* in the large and small elements of its form counters its fluidities and lightnesses with archaic flats, solids, and simplicities. As coordinate terms in critical analysis, "archaic" and "Hellenistic" are perhaps not very satisfactory, and they tend to bury a live play in its history. One might rather use an equivalent but timeless pair of terms, "Strength" and "Grace." They are primary in the thought of G. M. Hopkins, used by Dryden in describing Congreve, and can be found in both Horace and Virgil as *virtus et venus*. The extremes of both Strength and Grace in combination may have been a quite clear intention in the mind of Euripides, since the Bacchae themselves, Dionysus himself, and even Pentheus in his mad scene are that paradox incarnate.

SONG-MAKING

We know nothing about the music of this play except some instruments. The flute was the standard instrument of the Dionysus cult, the chorus describes its effect at some length, and it almost certainly accompanied much of the singing. Euripides speaks of the flute playing, in the sense of being *playful*. That would make it an element of Grace, though its register went fairly deep. His *playful* use of it would correspond to what seems to have been his predilection for trills or melisma, not to say "grace-notes." Against this he evidently used a deep and loud percussive instrument, a sort of drum, as an element of Strength. It is presumably carried by the chorus, but is not our familiar tambourine. It is much deeper and may be as big as the drum in the little mosaic by Dioskourides in the Naples Museum. In a sense these two instruments may be the stylistic key to the play.

SPECTACLE

Aristotle puts this element last, as belonging rather to scene and costume designers than to the poet, though he at least advises the poet to visualize the play while writing. Unhappily he has little to say on the subject, and classical theory in modern times has readily assumed that the theatrical side of drama should be kept very subordinate to more intellectual and ideal events. The relative staginess of Euripides is considered rather a decline into sensationalism and materialism. He is indeed more stagy than Sophocles, but not more than Aeschylus, whose showmanship is far gaudier and more violent, more massive, more architectural and sculptural as it were, and less pictorial and detailed. At present, or recently, we have been insisting on spectacle, on the sensational event, at the expense of the intellectual or "verbal" element, sometimes quite programmatically under Artaud's theory of cruelty. Not only the cast but the scenery invades the audience and includes it in an "environment." What used to be a stage designer is now an "environment consultant." On the other hand there is a distinct reaction backwards to drawing-room comedy that stays behind the proscenium and is all talk. This is a very immediate contemporary issue and not easily decided either at the box office or in theory.

It would be too easy—and unhistorical—to exclude the forms and feelings of the circus or the pageant or the Grand Guignol from tragic drama proper. You would have to exclude Aeschylus and Shakespeare as well as Euripides from tragedy, and be left with "classic" tragedy like some of Sophocles and some of Racine. Classic tragedy is a splendid kind of tragedy but certainly not all of tragedy nor even tragedy par excellence. It has the special intensity of concentration and exclusion, but the abundance of tragic reality and possibility cannot be contained in it or even subordinated to it. On the other hand, a purely or predominantly sensational theatre is quite as narrow, if as thrilling, or, in Aristotle's word, psychagogic; and even when it is as wonderful as a circus or a parade, one soon comes to miss what it fails to involve.

The Bacchae contains a great deal of broad and vivid stage business—the collapse of the palace, a flash of lightning or so, the epiphany of the god in a bull mask, as I have discussed them in the stage notes—but of course the most inordinate piece of sensationalism is the assembling of the body of

Pentheus by Agave. Ordinarily—whether or not by convention—Greek tragedy commits its atrocities off stage and is even rather discreet about the exhibition of bloody remains or of disfigured heroes like Oedipus, Hercules, and Hippolytus. We are indeed spared the dismemberment of the hero on stage, but the piecing together of the body limb by limb is the ghastliest business in all Greek tragedy, and up to the hopes of Antonin Artaud. It is monstrous, or seems so; and if so, Aristotle would exclude it from tragedy. Nietzsche probably would not, since he speaks of a "healthy" neurosis, the "need for the horrible." If one has that kind of health and does feel a need for the horrible, and if the satisfaction of a need is a pleasure, one might argue that an extreme of physical horror provides extreme pleasure through one of "such feelings," one of the degrees of fear, and so is proper to tragedy. Historically, too, one has to admit several species of tragedy which batten on physical horror—the Senecan, the German Romantic as in Kleist if not Goethe, and indeed the Elizabethan and Jacobean. Other species of tragedy avoid horror: the French Classic, Ibsen, and most Greek—but in 406 B.C. we are on or past the threshold of Hellenistic sensationalism, so that gauging the intended degree of horror in the *compositio* is no simple operation, if possible at all. For practical purposes in a modern production, Cadmus can hold a cloth just high enough to conceal the members from the audience while Agave composes them, but this is more an evasion than a solution of the obvious problem.

At the worst, the *compositio* is not a simple case of the horrible. It has an admixture of pity. A late Greek rhetorician (Apsines, third century A.D.) refers to it twice as an

example of pity—Agave rouses pity by her allocutions to the
several parts. One cannot trust a late scholar on such a point,
as he may never have seen the play and can easily discount
the awful visual presence of the bloody and mangled limbs
throughout the scene, yet he may be right, and I would say
the scene has a very high potential of pity to be exploited by
the actress, who had better be a strong one. Negotiating the
emotions of the scene and those of an audience in sympathy
with it is delicate, and fending off hysteria or revulsion is
not easy. One might suppose the natural reaction of the
heroine at this juncture would be to go mad, but Agave has
just recovered from her happy state of madness and now
stays nothing but sane and sober, and speaks, so far as one can
tell from the remaining scraps of text, in straight iambics,
when one would expect at least a more agitated metric. She
has already sung in a highly agitated metric in her first
passage with the chorus, and her terrible steadiness now
helps to keep the audience steady. This could not, I think,
be done without having the agitated passage and madness
behind us, emphatically disposed of but still in mind. Also,
Agave has been demonstrated as a powerful woman, as it
were a primitive or "feudal" aristocrat, so she is capable,
even without the supernatural strength of Dionysiac possession, of putting her son's body together with her own mur-
derous hands. The pity of the audience is not for a merely
pathetic woman but for an admirable and heroic one. Her
being equal to the task helps make the audience equal to
watching it. There is a streak of Clytemnestra in her, and
indeed the whole moral power and largeness of the scene
is more Aeschylean than Euripidean. But I doubt that a
similar scene existed in the earlier plays by Aeschylus.

Still the scene has its horrible visual side and is dangerously close to comedy. Agave asks, "Who is this man whose
corpse I hold in hand?" It is a natural question, because the
head is missing, but it comes with a hair's breadth of
Galgenhumor, which would be excellent in Kleist or Büchner
or Artaud or even Seneca, but not in Euripides, even this
late, and above all not at this moment in the play. Agave is
now in her right mind and perfectly serious. But how is the
audience to feel? The identification of dismembered bodies
is a daily problem on our highways and on battlefields, but
not many of the audience can be expected to have engaged in
it, or seen it done, or even imagined it in detail. Even the
washing and laying out of corpses in good repair is not
common experience any more. In Athens it certainly was,
and at nearly the end of the long Peloponnesian War, which
went in for massacres by hand, the physical part of this
scene would not have seemed far-fetched or even "absurd."
It could probably be played at full strength. The danger of
losing the audience because of disbelief in a dismembered
dummy or calf is lessened by the distance of the corpse from
the audience and its supine position. In any case the visibil-
ity can be adjusted to the "needs" of a particular audience.
The real danger is in losing the audience through revulsion
or distracting it from the emotional content of the scene by
a sadistic thrill.

The subjectivity of any member or indeed the collective
subjectivity of the audience would react to the simple exhibition of such a corpse in a number of subjective ways—
with revulsion, ghoulish pleasure, or determination to endure
the sight. Or it would react objectively, saying "Nonsense,
that's a dummy," or again, "That's the way it is. I saw the

same thing on the turnpike, or at Melos." But in the theatre
the subjectivity of the audience is not itself, not alone with
the object; it is committed, loosely or tightly, to the sub-
jectivities of the characters. The situation is one of intersubjectivity, a highly variable and delicate relation, but a
prime relation of drama, if not of all the arts. The audience
does not identify with Agave, having the same feelings of
guilt and desperate grief. If that were possible, it would
still be a transposition of subjectivity, not intersubjective,
and certainly no "pleasure." The subjectivity of the audience
is sufficiently distinct from hers to feel a pity for her which
she does not feel for herself, but is still in sympathy or
harmony with her grief, which is the controlling emotion.
The dramatist's problem is how to keep it in control of the
intersubjective situation, in the midst of potential horror,
distraction, hysteria, comedy. One great means of control,
though not infallible or sufficient in itself, is to keep the
emotion articulate—the mere actuality of Agave's voice
expressing her grief (and in steady iambics) goes far to pre-
occupy the attention of the audience and give her grief
precedence or command over other feelings which are potential but inarticulate. The intersubjective feelings about the
parts of the body she addresses are thus predominantly hers
—maternal tenderness, doting admiration, regret and so on
—not those of the audience in direct relation to it. Even so,
the emotions of the audience, at this intensity, could get
out of control or insubordinate. Instead of pity, it may simply
feel her situation and her feelings are totally unendurable,
and stop listening. But the audience is not alone with Agave
and the corpse; Cadmus is there, a pitying as well as a
grieving presence, whether he is speaking or silent. Our

feeling for Agave is stabilized by our feeling with him for her. He is in a way the salvation of the scene, establishing its intersubjective equilibrium above the visual horror.

I think the scene must have worked in some such way, but since most of it is lost, enough.